Alternatives

A Family Guide to Legal and Financial Planning for the Disabled

This publication is designed to provide accurate and authoritative information in regard to the subject matter covered. It is sold with the understanding that the publisher and the author are not engaged in rendering legal, accounting or other professional service. If legal advice or other expert assistance is required, the services of a competent professional person should be sought.

Alternatives

A Family Guide to Legal and Financial Planning for the Disabled

L. Mark Russell

First Publications, Inc., P.O. Box 1832
Evanston, Illinois 60204

Library of Congress Number: 83-80131
Printed in the United States of America
© 1983 by L. Mark Russell. All rights reserved.
Published in 1983.
ISBN 0-912891-00-9

Editors: Catherine L. Caldwell, Doug Utigard
Design: John Reuter-Pacyna

FIRST PUBLICATIONS INC., P.O. Box 1832
Evanston, Illinois 60204

To: My Parents

The author acknowledges the substantial contributions of Amy
K. Dixon, Marla Desnet Zelikow and Katherine Smith Dedrick in
the research, writing and development of this book.

I want to express my gratitude to Leo Kneer, as friend, teacher,
editor, and consultant. To Suzanne M. Joseph for her work on the
financial chapter which is an outgrowth of her considerable
experience advising families with disabled children. To Robert
Hodgson, member of the New York State Bar, and John M.
Skalla who served as critical readers for portions of this book. To
Gloria Hoover who flawlessly typed the manuscript. To Field
Graphics, Inc. for typesetting and keylining the material. To
Fairfield Graphics for printing the book.

Contents

Introduction

All families need to make legal and financial plans for the future. Because of their special needs, families with mentally disabled children must plan even more carefully than others. For them the planning must start sooner, last longer, and take more details into consideration. For this reason, the primary intent of this book is to make the estate planning process understandable and to simplify parents' efforts to provide security for their children now and in the future.

Alternatives presents, in one clear and comprehensive volume, the basic elements of estate planning with emphasis on the special needs of families with mentally disabled relatives. The term "mentally disabled" is used here to describe both the mentally ill and the mentally retarded. The range of estate planning topics includes wills, guardianship, trusts, maximizing governmental benefits for the disabled, taxes, insurance, and financial planning.

Although *Alternatives* has been written specifically with mentally disabled individuals in mind, some of the information will also apply to the physically disabled. In addition, because it is a comprehensive source of this specialized information, this book is a useful reference guide for professionals—lawyers, social workers, and administrators of services and organizations for the mentally handicapped.

Because of its special focus, *Alternatives* will answer many of the urgent questions parents have:

- Does my child need a legal guardian?

- Can I control who will be the guardian of my child when I die?

- How can I give money to my disabled child without jeopardizing eligibility for government benefits and exposing this money to collection by the government?

● Am I taking advantage of all the possible medical deductions and credits that I am entitled to receive?

● Will the proceeds from my life insurance policy actually reduce my child's financial resources? If so, how can I correct that problem?

● What is the easiest way of obtaining medical insurance for my handicapped child? What provisions should I look for in the policy?

"Estate planning" is not an activity for only the wealthy. Parents must plan their estates, regardless of size, to secure the continual care and independence of the disabled child. Estate planning should be broadly viewed to include both financial and personal planning. All parents need to consider whether or not a guardian is needed for their mentally disabled child now or after their deaths. Familes with limited financial resources must learn to maximize government benefits and stretch the value of their money by taking advantage of the available medical tax deductions and credits, by choosing the most effective medical insurance for the disabled person, by getting the most out of their life insurance, by knowing why trusts can be so practical for families who rely on government benefits, by investing prudently, and so forth. This book, in fact, assumes that most families' financial resources are limited and that they are forced to plan their estates very carefully in order to achieve maximum care and independence for the disabled person.

Although there are many *alternatives* that all parents of the disabled should consider, there is no single magic formula for creating the appropriate estate plan. Every estate plan should be custom-fit to the family circumstances and the needs of the disabled person. For instance, the nature and degree of the child's disability will determine the need and type of guardianship. The wealth of a family effects tax planning and the reliance on government benefits for the disabled person. The number of children in a family might influence the distribution of assets in a will or a trust. In other words, estate planning is a process of weighing numerous alternatives and making decisions that you hope will improve and secure your child's life now and in the future.

To be assured of having a sound plan, it is very important to select an attorney carefully. This book is not intended to replace the attorney in the estate planning process. Professional legal advice is always needed because laws change and because no one book can address the unique circumstances of every family. Moreover, the laws in each state vary.

It is important to find an attorney with an awareness of estate planning and an appreciation for the special problems created by the child's disability. Most lawyers have not been exposed to the legal questions affecting families with mentally disabled children, and consequently are unaware of much of the specialized information contained in this book. For this reason, parents should consider sharing this information with their attorneys. This may provide the attorney with helpful direction and consequently may save both time and money.

If an attorney is not familiar with the planning for the disabled, he or she may make some critical, though unintentional, errors in preparing the plan. For instance, if a typical trust format is used for a disabled individual, the state government might collect the trust property in repayment for benefits received by the disabled individual. Such a trust might also make the disabled individual ineligible for current government benefits. There are certain trusts that may eliminate these problems, but without the particular information from this book or from extensive research, an attorney could formulate an inadequate plan.

Parents should be open, direct, and explicit with an attorney about the degree and type of their child's disability. The nature of the disability will determine the many facets of the estate plan such as whether or not a guardian is needed and if so what type is most suitable. The more information parents give, the more certain the family can be of meeting its estate planning goals.

Parents may find a lawyer who specializes in estate planning for the disabled by asking other parents of mentally disabled children for references. People who have already been through the estate planning process may be willing to share recommendations about attorneys, as well as information about legal costs and special planning problems they encountered and solved. Another resource for finding a qualified attorney is the local or state unit of the National Association for Retarded Citizens or any other mental health organization. If these organizations cannot help, parents can check lawyer referral services and state and local bar associations. The telephone directory will have listings of these groups.

It is important to discuss the attorney's fee at the initial consultation, before hiring. A lawyer may be willing to offer group rates if the client belongs to an association for parents of disabled children and can bring other members' business. While it is natural to want to pay the lowest possible legal fees, parents should place the greater emphasis on an attorney's special knowledge and experience in estate planning for the disabled.

Remember that this book is not intended to be the only resource tool in estate planning for the disabled. Laws and requirements about estate planning methods are changing constantly. It is therefore necessary to check all your plans closely with an attorney before they become final. Once a plan is made it should be periodically evaluated and revised to guarantee the maximum possible care for the disabled in light of new legal requirements. Moreover, when developing your estate plan you should consult not only a lawyer, but discuss your plans with your family and the disabled person, and with experts in the mental health field. Although there can be no guarantee that an estate plan will provide lifelong care and protection for a disabled person, a plan is essential for parents who are concerned about what will happen to their children now and after the parents are gone.

Chapter 1
Wills

Nobody likes to think about writing a will because it is an acknowledgement of death. But writing a will is essential if your property is to be distributed the way you intend it. If you do not write a will, or if you have a legally invalid will, you will lose control over the distribution of your property and over your entire estate plan.

Through a will you can control not only what happens to your property, but you can select who will take care of your minor and/or disabled children after your death. For this reason, parents of the mentally disabled should write a will regardless of their age or wealth. Moreover, almost everyone has a larger estate at their death than they realize. Many parents own a home, and most parents with mentally disabled children own life insurance. With just these two assets, writing a will is crucial.

Your will should answer three basic questions:

1. How should your property be distributed?
2. Who should take care of your minor and/or disabled children?
3. Who will carry out the terms of your will?

Just "putting it in writing" does not guarantee that your wishes will be carried out; your will must comply with several legal requirements. These legal requirements will be understood only by a lawyer practicing in your state. For that reason it is important that you contact a lawyer to draft your will.

This chapter will discuss what will happen to your estate plan and the security of your disabled child if you do not have a will, when it is appropriate to disinherit your disabled child, how and when you need to name a guardian in your will to protect your minor and/or disabled child after your death, what elements to include in your will, and finally, what will happen if a mentally disabled person owns property and needs to write a will.

WHAT WILL HAPPEN IF YOU DO NOT HAVE A WILL?

If you die without a will, the state will write one for you. The state will distribute your property according to its probate laws. These laws are designed for the general public and do not consider the special problems faced by families with mentally disabled children.

The state laws may distribute the property equally among the surviving children. If a family has a small estate they might want to give their property to other children and have the disabled person rely on government aid. Or, the family might want a portion of the inheritance to go into a trust for the benefit of the disabled child. Or, the family might want more assets to go to their disabled child than to their other children. But without a will parents have no choices; they lose control over the distribution of their property and are unable to name a guardian in their will to care for their child after their death.

The big mistake. Whether you have a will or not, the biggest estate planning mistake you may make is to allow your mentally disabled child to inherit or receive a large amount of cash or other assets. Whenever money or cash-like assets are received by a mentally disabled person in situations such as when the parents die without a will, when they bequest money to their disabled child under their will, when they give money as a gift to their disabled child, or when a trust is improperly drafted for a disabled beneficiary, four basic problems can occur.

First, the receipt of money in any of these ways might reduce or terminate the handicapped person's governmental benefits. These benefits are often relied upon by families to reduce the tremendous costs—averaging $30,000 annually—of providing private care for the disabled. Many of the government programs, both state and federal, have eligibility requirements that participants must meet to qualify for the benefits. Generally, if the disabled person is over 18 years of age, these eligibility requirements consider the net worth and income of only the disabled person rather than the whole family's net worth or income. Therefore, if the parents do not have a will and their disabled child inherits their property according to state laws, the child may not benefit at all due to the reduction or termination of governmental aid such as Supplemental Security Income (SSI) or Medicaid.

The second problem connected with the disabled person receiving money or cash-like assets is that some state laws mandate the state to seize the money to pay for current or past services rendered to the disabled person. This type of law is becoming more popular among the states as their economic problems increase. The states seek reimbursements from those recipients who can "afford" to pay, to lessen the burden on other taxpayers. These states do not want to maintain a public charity for all mentally disabled persons. For example, in Illinois the Mental Health Code decrees that a disabled person who is a recipient of state mental health or developmental disability services must pay the state for all *current and past* services if he or she has the resources to pay. As soon as the disabled person has received the money, he or she has the resources to pay and must surrender them.

The third problem associated with the disabled person receiving money is that he or she generally will not be able to manage the money and the court might appoint a guardian of the estate for this purpose. The guardian of the estate will be appointed by the court to manage, spend, and invest the disabled person's money for his or her benefit.

As discussed in more detail in the guardianship chapter, the appointment of a guardian of the estate may cause many problems: your child may have to be ruled incompetent, there may be fees, the posting of a bond, restrictive investment rules, and complicated approval procedures for expenditures. In short, this is a consequence that should not happen through neglect or inadvertence.

The fourth problem is that the disabled person will have to plan what happens to the assets after his or her own death. This may involve writing a will. The special problems involved when a mentally disabled person writes a will are discussed at the end of this chapter.

For all of these reasons, families must plan their estates together. If the family relies on governmental benefits, the disabled person should not inherit money or cash-like assets from anyone —the grandparents, uncles or aunts, brothers or sisters, or close friends. Everyone should be so informed.

As just mentioned, when disabled people inherit money a number of these problems can occur. To avoid these problems, it is often better to disinherit your disabled child under your will, and leave money in a trust for the disabled child's benefit. As will be discussed in the trust chapter, unlike wills and gifts, trusts can allow you to give money for the benefit of your disabled child without causing a reduction or termination of government benefits or collection of the disabled person's assets by government creditors. Furthermore, a trustee can serve the same function a guardian of the estate does without having to comply with all the court requirements.

DISINHERITANCE

Disinheriting your handicapped child—that is, leaving no money to the disabled person by way of will, trust, or gift—will help avoid direct inheritance problems. This technique is primarily used by families with small estates. Such a family realizes that its resources cannot adequately provide for the costly needs of the disabled person. These families would rather have the disabled person rely on the government for care and maintenance and give their small estates to their other children. These families are not indifferent toward their disabled child; rather, they have chosen a realistic plan in light of their small resources.

If you feel disinheriting your child will hurt his or her feelings (or hurt *your* feelings), especially when other children are receiving bequests, you can leave a token bequest so the child feels loved. To avoid eligibility problems, this bequest should be less than $1,000. There is no legal problem with regard to disinheriting your child, because no state except Louisiana requires parents to provide post-death support for their children.

Disinheritance can have its disadvantages. When the family disinherits the handicapped person, they often give their assets to another child with the understanding that this child will care for and protect the disabled child. However, this child is not *legally bound* to spend money on behalf of the disabled person. In addition, a financial emergency might force the healthy child to spend the inheritance. For these reasons, parents should not rely on these types of understandings to provide for the future security of the disabled person.

Another disadvantage of disinheritance is that the handicapped person's well-being and comfort depend solely on government benefits, which may be inadequate. Moreover, these government benefits are subject to political cut-backs in funding. But, for families with few resources, these risks must often be taken.

Total disinheritance should be distinguished from partial disinheritance. Families totally disinherit the disabled person when they leave no money or property to the disabled person by any means—by will, by gift, or by trust. Families partially disinherit the disabled person when, for example, they leave no assets to the disabled person by will or gift, but put money into a trust that benefits their child. Often, a good estate plan for a medium-income family who relies on government funds is to disinherit their child by bequesting no money to their child by will, but to set up a "supplemental benefits" trust as discussed in the trust chapter. This type of trust can provide comfort that is supplemental to government aid without exposing the trust assets to governmental creditors and may avoid causing any reduction or termination of the disabled person's governmental benefits.

When you want to disinherit your handicapped child, leave the child no legacy under your will. However, to completely disinherit your child this is not enough. Most wills cannot designate who will receive each and every belonging constituting your property. All property not named in your will is distributed according to state probate laws. These laws give a portion of this left-over property to your disabled child, again causing eligibility problems. To avoid this problem, your will should contain a "residuary clause." The residuary clause designates the beneficiaries to the left-over property that is not specifically named in your will. In this way, you can be assured of safely excluding your disabled child from your will.

TESTAMENTARY GUARDIANS

Even though you decide to disinherit your disabled child you are not abandoning your child or withholding the support and care he or she will need after your death. The financial support will be provided by government benefit programs and/or by property in a trust you establish. The care and guidance of the disabled person can also be arranged through the appointment of a personal and/or estate guardian. Several questions naturally come to parents' minds in this situation, including

● Who will care for our child after our deaths?

● How can we control today the selection of a person who will have legal authority to care for our child after we are gone?

Possibly, the answer to providing a continuity of care for the future security of your child will be to name a *testamentary guardian* in your will. The guardian is called a "testamentary" guardian because he or she is named in your will rather than appointed while you are alive. As will be discussed in the guardianship chapter, a guardian has legal authority to make decisions for your child in the areas of personal care or financial matters or both. The naming of a testamentary guardian in your will is your control over who will care for your minor and/or disabled child. If you have not nominated someone as guardian for a child who needs a guardian, the court must select one without knowing your preferences.

If your child needs a guardian (establishing this need will be discussed in the guardianship chapter) you will probably want to fill this role during your lifetime. But you will also want to select future guardians to provide protection for your child after your death. The way to select a person or organization to be guardian, *if your state permits it*, is to name a "successor guardian" in the court order which establishes the original guardianship. A successor guardian takes the place of another guardian who can no longer perform the duties.

However, if your state does not permit you to name a successor guardian in the original guardianship order, then ask your lawyer if your state allows you to name a testamentary guardian. Most states permit some form of successor or testamentary guardian. In some states, such as Illinois, *only parents who have been appointed legal guardians* can nominate a valid testamentary guardian for their adult disabled child in their will. (Parents of a minor child are presumed to be the child's guardians.) The testamentary guardian must notify the court of the death or incapacity of the original guardian, and the court must approve the selection of the testamentary guardian. Most courts are delighted to approve the parents' selection of a guardian to provide continuity of care for the disabled child.

To insure that your minor and/or disabled child will have the protection of a guardian throughout his or her lifetime, try to select a testamentary guardian (and successor guardians as well) who might live as long as your disabled child. To further guarantee life-long guardianship protection, name more than one testamentary guardian in your will. If more than one guardian is named, be sure that you clearly indicate the order in which the guardians assume the guardianship appointment. In choosing a testamentary guardian, as in choosing any guardian, match the capabilities of the guardian with the unique needs of the disabled person.

GUIDELINES FOR CREATING A WILL

It is important that you consult an attorney when you draft a will. Your attorney will know the legal requirements for a valid will in your particular state. Each state has different requirements. For instance, some states require two witnesses while others require three witnesses. Some states permit hand written wills; others do not. Never attempt to write a will without an attorney.

Without the aid of an attorney your will might fail to comply with the state's legal requirements. If it does not follow the legal requirements, the probate court will declare your will invalid. If this happens, you have lost control over your estate, and the security of your child may be jeopardized.

Another problem with a self-drafted will is that its validity tends to be challenged in probate court. Your estate may pay the attorney fees when your will has to be defended in court. A battle in probate court can drain your entire estate. And, again, if your will loses in court, your wishes will be ignored.

Before you retain an attorney to draft your will, there are several things you should think about in advance. Working out some of the details before you meet with your attorney can save you time and money and can, in the long run, result in a better document. Prior to drafting your will:

- Discuss with your family the objectives you want to achieve.

- Make a list of your major assets, such as your house, car, stocks, insurance.

- Choose your beneficiaries. That is, decide whom you wish to receive your assets. At this point you must decide whether or not to leave any assets to your disabled child. Unless you are not concerned about maintaining government benefits for your child, in most cases your options include

    1. Disinheriting your disabled child, either totally or partially;

2. Giving your child a token legacy that will not jeopardize benefits, or:

3. Giving your child assets that are exempt from his or her net worth when eligibility for government programs is determined. Examples of exempt assets might include a house or a car, but they vary from program to program.

• Select alternate beneficiaries to receive the assets.

• Decide if you want to name a testamentary guardian for your disabled child, and if so, decide who it should be and secure that person's willingness to serve. Be sure your state law permits the appointment of a testamentary guardian.

• Select the person who will be responsible for distributing your assets to the beneficiaries and secure that person's willingness to serve. This person is called an executor. When selecting your executor keep in mind the important responsibilities he or she will have:

1. To assemble and inventory your property;

2. To pay your funeral expenses;

3. To file estate and income tax returns;

4. To sell your property if necessary to pay your outstanding bills or to make the proper distributions as described in your will;

5. To submit a "final accounting" to the probate court. This final accounting is due after the administration of the estate has been completed. In it the executor shows the court that all bills have been paid and the property is ready to be distributed;

6. To distribute the property according to your will.

Letter of Intent. At the same time you write the will you should consider writing a Letter of Intent. A Letter of Intent is a document, usually attached to the will, which expresses the parents' preferences for the type of care the disabled person is to receive after the parents' death. Although the Letter of Intent does not bind anyone legally, it can guide the future guardian, trustee, relatives, and others who will be responsible for caring for your child. For example, you might express in the Letter of Intent your desire for your child eventually to leave the large institutional residential facility where he or she currently resides and move into a supervised group home and subsequently move into an independent apartment. In it you should state the general characteristics of the type of care you hope your child will receive.

After your will has been drafted there are several things to remember:

• Leave a copy of your will with your attorney and keep a copy yourself. Avoid placing your copy of the will in a safety deposit box, because upon your death the box may be temporarily sealed.

• Regularly review your will. Ask yourself the following questions:

Have your estate planning objectives changed?

Has the size of your estate dramatically changed?

Has a law changed that warrants a change in your will?

• Consult an attorney if you decide to change your will. Do not write on your will, erase any portion of it, or alter it in any way. If you want to change your will, have your attorney draft a new will or add a "codicil" to the will. A codicil is a formally executed addition to or change in the terms of a will, and does not require the complete rewriting of the will. For example, you might use a codicil rather than rewrite an entire new will if you have forgotten something or want to change one clause such as naming a testamentary guardian for your child.

In summary, *your will allows you to control your estate plan.* The will should be drafted by an attorney to insure its validity. If you thoughtfully consider the objectives of your will and estate plan, you can strengthen the future security of your disabled child.

WILLS WRITTEN BY THE MENTALLY DISABLED

As discussed earlier, most families want to avoid giving the disabled person property which he or she will be unable to manage and which will jeopardize government benefits. However, due to poor estate planning, sometimes the mentally disabled person has property and wishes to write a will. What are the the problems involved in this process?

One potential problem is that a will written by a mentally handicapped person may be challenged as invalid in probate court after the disabled person's death. The disabled person's estate will have to pay the attorney fees to defend the will. The attorney fees can drain the entire assets of the estate.

Whether or not the will is declared valid, assuming it was

drafted properly, will probably depend on the "testamentary capacity" of the disabled person at the time he or she signed the will. Testamentary capacity is the legal competence to make a will. Most states require that the maker of the will be of sound mind when the will is made. This is generally interpreted to mean that the disabled person does not need help in knowing how much property he or she has, in knowing that he or she is making a will, in knowing that family members exist who might benefit from the estate, and in knowing the consequences of the will and of signing it. Usually, the problem is not that the disabled person does not meet this legal standard. Rather, the problem is that whenever a mentally disabled person makes a will it begs to be challenged in probate court, and this results in costly litigation.

Chapter 2
Guardianship

Appointing a guardian is another alternative which may further secure your mentally disabled child's future. Mentally disabled people can be vulnerable in society and need the protection of a guardian. The necessity of guardianship, the types of guardianship, and the alternatives to guardianship will be explored. Practical suggestions on obtaining a guardianship will be explained.

WHAT IS GUARDIANSHIP?

A guardian "guards" the mentally disabled person who because of a disability is incapable of caring for his or her person or estate. Unlike advisors, social workers, lawyers, and others trained to help the disabled, the guardian, appointed by a court, has legal powers to make decisions for a ward (the mentally disabled person). The decisions the guardian has the power to make vary, depending on the type of guardian appointed. It is the guardian's duty to assist the ward in the development of maximum self-reliance.

There are two basic types of guardians—guardians of the person and guardians of the estate. A guardian responsible for the personal care of the mentally disabled individual is called a guardian of the person. The guardian of the person may make decisions for the ward concerning, for example, residential placement, medical and psychiatric care, education, vocational training, food, clothing, comfort, and other personal affairs. The second type of guardian, called a guardian of the estate in many states, is responsible for managing the ward's financial matters and preserving the ward's estate. This guardian can make decisions that may range from how the disabled person's money is invested to paying the ward's bills. The same person can serve both the personal and financial functions. Again, in some states, the types of guardians vary depending on the type of protection sought. These different types of guardians will be discussed in later sections.

WHY SHOULD PARENTS CONSIDER GUARDIANSHIP?

Throughout this chapter the term guardian will describe any person or organization who is legally appointed by a *court* to make decisions for your child. When your mentally disabled child legally becomes an adult, at the age of 18 in most states, it is necessary, *even though you are the parent,* to apply legally to become your adult child's guardian, if that person is incapable of making essential personal and financial decisions and therefore needs a guardian.

Since *any* person reaching adulthood is presumed by the state to be competent, no other persons, including the person's parents, may legally make decisions on his or her behalf. This is true even if a mental health agency or social service agency has determined for its programs that the person is mentally handicapped. An adult individual is presumed competent unless a *court* formally appoints someone as guardian.

As parents you may have agreed with each other or with friends and relatives to continue to make decisions for your mentally disabled child after the child reaches adulthood. Legally, these private agreements are meaningless. Only a legally appointed guardian can legally make a decision for a person who has reached adulthood. Although the court's caution may seem unnecessary in cases where loving parents know what is best for their adult disabled child, by involving a judge in the process of appointing a guardian, the legal system ensures that disabled people's rights will not be harmed by the appointment of unnecessary guardians.

Generally, parents initiate the guardianship proceedings for their mentally disabled child, and usually the parents are the ones originally appointed as guardians. Even if you, as a parent, plan to be appointed guardian of your child, you need to consider the qualities of other people who could assume the guardianship appointment if you were unable to continue. Choosing a guardian to replace you when you die gives you an added measure of control over the future security of your adult disabled child. If your child needs a guardian after your death, and you have not selected a future guardian, a court may have to appoint a guardian without knowing your preferences. Throughout this chapter, pay particular attention to which factors to consider when choosing a guardian.

DOES MY CHILD NEED A GUARDIAN?

Essentially, a mentally disabled person needs a guardian if he or she cannot make sound decisions in regard in personal care and financial matters and *cannot communicate* to others that someone must make these decisions. Think objectively about your disabled child and ask yourself whether he or she understands *when* a decision needs to be made, the *alternatives* available in making a decision and, finally, the *consequences* of that decision. You should also analyze a variety of other factors such as the disabled person's functional level, socialization skills and the availability of other less restrictive alternatives. If a mental disability either partially or totally impairs the decision-making ability of a person, guardianship may be proper protection, depending on the types of guardianships available in your state.

When no guardian has been appointed for a mentally disabled person incapable of making decisions, the disabled person is in a "catch 22" situation in which no one can make critical decisions. The following example illustrates one problem that might occur if your mentally disabled child does not have the protection of a guardian. Some of the most important decisions adults make involve medical care. An adult needing surgery must sign a medical consent form. If the patient is mentally disabled, normally the physician requires the signature of a guardian.

Martha is a multiple-handicapped, mentally retarded adult. She is forty years old and lives in a group home that is supervised 24 hours a day.

At a quarterly physical examination, Martha is diagnosed as having an embolism in which a blood clot blocks one of her arteries. Martha is hospitalized for an operation. When the surgeon examines her, he realizes she is mentally retarded and is unable to legally consent to the operation.

Since Martha is a disabled adult, the surgeon calls Martha's parents and asks if they are her guardians and can they sign the consent-to-treatment form. The parents had not become Martha's guardian when she reached 18 years of age, and the operation is postponed. Immediately, the parents contact their lawyer to appear in court to obtain an emergency, temporary guardianship that gives the parents the power to consent to medical treatment for Martha. Fortunately, the parents are able to obtain an emergency, temporary guardianship and can give consent for all medical treatment before a serious delay in treatment results.

Martha's parents, like most, did not prevent foreseeable problems by becoming the permanent guardian of their adult disabled child. If Martha's parents were dead and there were no guardian, it might have taken even longer to find a guardian to consent to the operation.

Medical care is only one situation when a guardian can be helpful. Increasingly, both public and private residential facilities request the appointment of a guardian before admitting the disabled person into the facility. In some states, if your adult child resides in a state institution, the law does not require the institution to notify parents or relatives of programmatic and treatment matters concerning the disabled person *unless they are the guardians.* As parents or guardians you have the right to appeal institutional decisions that are not in the disabled person's best interests. However, unless you are the guardian of the adult disabled person, you may never find out about those decisions, because the institution may not be obligated to notify anyone except the guardian.

Another common function for which a guardian is needed is to obtain access to confidential records and files and to attend programmatic staff meetings concerning the disabled person. Many states have confidentiality laws which prevent anyone except the disabled person from obtaining confidential material about himself or herself. In addition, the mentally disabled person may not have the legal mental capacity required to release this information for concerned relatives to examine. To avoid this problem, particularly for a non-related person who will care for the disabled person after the parents' deaths, the guardianship order can grant the guardian the power to examine this confidential information.

These examples illustrate only a few of the powers the court can grant the guardian in the guardianship order. The laws vary from state to state concerning the types of guardianships available and how responsive they are to the unique needs of the ward. Flexibility in your state law may permit you to tailor the guardianship order to the specific needs of the disabled person. This flexibility may help to determine whether or not a guardian is appropriate. The guardianship which allows parents to custom-fit the responsibilities of the guardian to the needs of the disabled person, called a limited guardianship, will be discussed in an upcoming section.

WHO SHOULD BE A GUARDIAN?

In general, the laws in most states permit anyone to be court-appointed as guardian if he or she is an adult, is of sound mind, has never been convicted of a serious crime, and is found capable, by a judge, to be a guardian. Some states require the guardian to be a resident of the state in which the disabled person resides. Other states require same-state residency only for guardians of the estate.

Most states allow public agencies such as state guardianship services to become guardians. A minority of states permit private agencies providing active guardianship programs to be appointed as guardians. In addition, most courts will not appoint an organization as guardian if that organization provides services directly to the disabled person—such as a residential facility. This is a precaution against conflict of interest problems.

Anyone considered for guardianship appointment should care and feel responsible for the disabled person and understand the nature and degree of the person's disability, the special needs which stem from that disability, and the ways in which appropriate living and treatment services can be obtained. Usually, family members, relatives, and close friends make the best guardians. However, sometimes parents must rule out these people because of their geographical distance, constant travelling, career plans, or lack of maturity.

In addition to considering whether or not the potential guardian understands the responsibilities of being a guardian and is willing and competent to perform the duties of a guardian, parents should consider these additional factors when choosing their child's guardian:

● Will the person or organization be able to visit the ward frequently and be available in emergency situations?

● Is the person or organization free of conflicts of interests and always willing to act in the best interests of the ward?

● Can the person or organization serve as guardian for a long period of time?

● Is the person or organization capable of solving problems pragmatically?

● Does the person or organization have experience in dealing with everyday legal and financial problems—bill paying, investments, insurance, taxes, and so forth?

A person or organization who meets the above criteria and can answer "yes" to each of these questions should be able to make decisions that protect and benefit the adult disabled ward.

LAWS COMMON TO GUARDIANSHIPS

As mentioned earlier, usually one of the parents or both will be appointed the guardian of a child. If you are the guardian, you will also want to select a guardian to replace you after your death or incapacity. This section will discuss some of the laws common to guardianship; a later section will analyze the specific types of guardians.

Compensation of the guardian. If a parent is appointed guardian there is generally no charge for services, unless the family is attempting to reduce the child's resources so the child will become or remain eligible for governmental benefits. If the guardian is not the parent or a relative, a fee may be charged to compensate the guardian. Generally, the court permits a guardian to be paid for reasonable fees and necessary expenses. After approval by the court, such compensation is paid out of the disabled person's estate unless paid by someone else.

Liability of a guardian. Generally, a guardian is not liable for either the acts or debts of the disabled person. A guardian of an adult disabled person is not required to use personal funds to pay for the financial needs of the disabled person. Generally, the assets of the guardian, even the parents, should not affect the *adult* disabled person's eligibility for governmental benefits. However, the guardian will be financially and legally liable in a few very specific circumstances.

For instance, a guardian who promises that he or she will pay for goods and services for the disabled person may be liable for the cost of these goods and services purchased by the disabled person. Additionally, the guardian may be legally liable for the wrongdoing of the disabled person only if the guardian *directed* and *approved* of those acts in advance.

Duty to report. Generally, guardians must make at least annual reports to the court. All states require a financial report from a guardian of the estate; some states require a report from a personal guardian. The sections discussing the guardian of the estate and the person will examine these requirements in greater detail.

Co-guardianship. Co-guardianship exists when two or more people or organizations are individually appointed as guardians of your mentally disabled child. Depending on what is written in the guardianship order, on the death of one of the co-guardians, the full decision-making authority may transfer to the surviving guardian or to another person or organization.

There are two common situations in which co-guardians are appointed. First, whenever one person is appointed guardian of the person and another person is appointed guardian of the estate for the same individual, the two guardians are considered co-guardians. In this case, they are not required to consult each other, although they should, and are not required to approve each other's decisions. If possible, it is highly recommended that one person serve both functions. The second situation arises when two individuals are appointed to share one guardianship. Often, both parents will be appointed or two siblings will be appointed as co-guardians for the disabled person. Before a decision can be made affecting the disabled ward, both guardians will have to agree on the course of action. The advantage of this is that it provides informed decision-making and a good check and balance, particularly when money is involved. The disadvantage is that a stalemate may occur between co-guardians, and a decision which should be made is postponed.

Generally, the decision to allow co-guardians is up to the judge hearing the guardianship proceeding. Normally, it is recommended to have one person or organization as guardian. However, exceptions arise when co-guardians need to be appointed to prevent potential conflict of interests, particulary when control of the disabled person's money is at stake.

TYPES OF GUARDIANS

As mentioned earlier, guardians can be classified into two categories according to whether they make decisions regarding the personal care of the ward (guardian of the person) or the financial care of the ward (guardian of the estate). In addition to the common characteristics previously explained, each type of guardianship has its own unique characteristics. The following sections will explain the different types of guardians, their function, and their characteristics.

Guardian of the person. Subject to the specific court order, a guardian of the person is responsible for the personal welfare of the disabled individual. The guardian's responsibilities may vary greatly. A guardian of the person may have to make decisions concerning the ward's residence, medical care, education, vocational development, food, clothing, leisure activities, attaining needed professional services, and so forth. If the ward has children, the guardian of the person may be given custody over them as well.

Some states require the guardian of the person to submit a report at least once a year. The report form varies from state to state. Normally, the report will briefly discuss the following:

• The current mental, physical, and social condition of the ward.

• The present living arrangement of the ward, and a description and address of every residence where the ward has lived during the period of guardianship, and the length of stay at each place.

• The medical, educational, vocational, and other professional services given to the ward.

• A summary of the guardian's visits and activities on behalf of the ward.

• Whether or not there is a need for continued guardianship.

• Other relevant information.

Although a guardian of the person may have broad authority, there are some decisions that are too personal for a substitute decision maker to control. For instance, the guardian generally does not have the right to draft the ward's will, consent to or veto a ward's marriage, decide whom a ward will vote for, or to donate a ward's organs after death. Currently, a very controversial issue is whether a guardian may make the decision to terminate a ward's life support system. In addition, most states will not allow a guardian to consent to health procedures which are intrusive on the person's body, such as sterilization, or to medical procedures which induce convulsions.

Furthermore, some states, such as Illinois and Washington, provide safeguards against involuntary commitments to a mental facility. These states allow wards to commit themselves voluntarily to mental facilities, but prevent the disabled person from being involuntarily commited without a hearing. Commitments in these states are treated as "involuntary" whenever the disabled person protests the commitment. In addition, in some states the guardianship order must *specifically* grant the guardian of the person the authority to admit a ward into a residential facility.

The guardian of the person is responsible for protecting the best interests of the disabled person. If your child needs help in making decisions about his or her personal care, you should consider selecting a guardian at least for after your death. (See Testamentary and Successor Guardians later in this chapter.) Carefully review the qualifications of each person you consider for guardianship appointment.

Guardian of the estate. Subject to the specific court order, a guardian of the estate is a person or organization appointed by the court to care for, manage, and invest the ward's property, with the duty to protect and preserve the property. The guardian of the estate must apply the principal and income of the estate for the ward's care, health, and comfort. A personal guardian may be sufficient for a disabled person with few resources. However, a guardian of the estate should be considered if the disabled person possesses substantial assets and is not competent to manage and invest those assets.

It is the duty of the guardian of the estate to use the assets only for the benefit of the ward and not for the guardian's personal profit. Unlike a trustee, the guardian of the estate does not have legal title to the ward's property; rather the guardian has a duty to manage the property. The guardian of the estate *should not commingle* or *combine* the ward's property or funds with his or her own property.

The legal system has established a standard of competence for the guardian of the estate. To meet this standard the estate guardian must use reasonable care and skill in managing the ward's financial affairs. Reasonable care and skill is normally defined as the care and skill that a person of ordinary prudence would exercise with personally owned property. If the guardian of the estate does the best he or she can do but still performs below the standard of a hypothetical person, the guardian has breached the duty of reasonable care.

There is a major qualification to this standard of care. The ordinary prudent person will take risks with a certain percentage of his or her own income, but the guardian of the estate is not permitted to take undue risks with the ward's property. The estate guardian is a *conservor* of assets. For example, a guardian may invest a ward's assets in U.S. Treasury securities in order to earn income safely, but cannot bet the money in Las Vegas for a quick return. The estate guardian might even breach his or her duty by investing the money in higher-risk growth stock companies.

In many states, to insure the guardian of the estate manages the ward's property competently and safely, the guardian is not permitted to spend or invest any of the ward's funds without first obtaining permission from the court. If a guardian spends the ward's money without prior court approval, the guardian may be charged for that money from personal funds.

To obtain court approval, with the help of a lawyer the guardian must petition the court for authority to make expenditures. The petition must state the purpose and amount of the proposed expenditure. The petition may be for one specific expenditure or the court may approve a number of expected transactions such as for rent, food, or clothing prior to the time they are actually needed. This procedure for obtaining court permission for expenditures results in considerable paperwork and inconvenience and could possibly delay payments which in some instances could harm the ward. It is one of the unavoidable disadvantages of having a guardian of the estate.

Similarly, many states require the guardian of the estate to obtain permission before investing the ward's property. All guardians of the estate have a duty to invest the ward's property. In some states, if the guardian allows the ward's money to remain uninvested in his or her possession, the court will charge the guardian interest on the uninvested money. Some courts do not require court permission to invest the ward's money in U.S. securities such as U.S. Treasury Bills. But states and judges vary. Many judges prefer that the investment be insured, which would rule out uninsured money market accounts. Some judges forbid a guardian to invest the ward's assets in equities such as real estate, even though such as investment may provide a hedge against inflation. Most judges prefer that the invested money yield higher income than it would in a pass-book savings account, preferring it to be in an account such as a fund that buys U.S. Treasury securities. Because states and judges vary, the guardian must get approval for the investment from the judge.

Although having a guardian of the estate can be helpful in protecting the ward's financial affairs, there can also be some definite disadvantages to having one. Two disadvantages have just been mentioned:

1. The paperwork necessary to obtain court permission for all expenditures made on behalf of the ward can be time-consuming and cumbersome; and

2. Restrictions designed to protect the assets may be too conservative for productive money management. Furthermore, though a relative who becomes a guardian may not charge a fee, an unrelated guardian can be expensive. This expense is paid from the disabled person's assets unless some other arrangement is made. It may be unwise to pay for financial expertise that cannot be fully used because of conservative investment restrictions.

Another expense related to the guardian of the estate that most states require is the posting of a bond. A bond is backed up by an amount of money which must be forfeited if the guardian makes a mistake or misdeed in the financial management of the ward's estate. Such bonds are sometimes called "performance" or "surety" bonds, and certain companies or individuals (bondsmen) specialize in guaranteeing payment of these bonds in case of forfeiture. Usually, the guardian must post a bond between one and one-half times the value of the personal estate of the ward depending upon the state and whether a surety company or an individual acts as surety. However, the guardian puts up a fraction of this amount to pay for the bond.

In some states, such as Illinois, Maine, Montana, and West Virginia, a judge has discretion to waive the bond requirement. In these states, the bond requirement is usally omitted when either the assets of the ward are minimal (less than $3000), or when the guardian of the estate is a bank.

Finally, most states require a guardian of the estate to submit detailed reports (called "accounts" or "accountings") to the court about the management and expenditures of the ward's money. To account for financial transactions is to provide a written statement of money earned, accrued, spent, and invested and to explain how and why these transactions have taken place. The guardian of the estate must account for every transaction made with the ward's money, and the receipts and cancelled checks must be attached. Normally the account is submitted to the court once a year, although each state's requirement differs. Furthermore, some courts require oral reports to supplement the written reports.

In light of the cost, reporting and paperwork requirements, as well as the investment and expenditure restrictions, a trust usually is a better alternative to fulfilling the parents' objectives. However, each family's situation is unique. Some families may want the safeguard of the court's watchful eye on the person responsible for managing the disabled person's finances. The pros and cons of a guardianship of the estate should be measured against the alternatives available, the family's objectives, and the needs of the disabled person.

Plenary vs limited guardian. The terms *plenary* and *limited* describe the extent or amount of decision-making authority the guardian has according to the guardianship order. The terms can be applied to either a guardian of the person or a guardian of the estate.

Plenary guardian: Virtually no limitations are placed on the decision-making authority of the plenary guardian. In many states, a plenary guardian (frequently called a "full" guardian or a "conservator") has decision-making authority over both the personal and financial aspects of the disabled ward's life. However, in other states, the term refers to the decision-making power of a guardian of the person or a guardian of the estate. For example, a plenary guardian of the person could make decisions concerning *all* aspects of the disabled ward's personal well-being (as opposed to his or her financial well-being)—food, clothing, health residence and so forth. A plenary guardianship is most appropriate for a *severely* disabled person who is completely without capacity to make or communicate responsible decisions about personal care or finances and needs the full protection of a guardian.

Many states appoint only plenary guardians. Because of the extensive powers of these guardians, usually a disabled adult must be declared totally incompetent before a plenary guardian can be appointed, even though the disability might not justify the declaration. The guardianship might be necessary, but a finding of total incompetency is unfortunate. (It should be noted that in some states such as New York, Colorado, and West Virginia, it is not necessary to declare the disabled person totally incompetent before appointing a plenary guardian. In these states, the ward of a plenary guardian can retain and enjoy basic privileges.)

If a plenary guardian is appointed, a chance exists that the disabled person will be deprived of the individual responsibility necessary for human growth. If the appointed guardian is sensitive to the disabled person's needs and skills, the guardian will encourage the person to be self-reliant and independent. But sensitive or insensitive, the appointed guardian completely controls the degree of responsibility and rights allowed the ward. The disabled ward may lose many rights such as the right to choose residential and educational services, the right to contract (for example, for a loan, or sign a lease), the right to manage money earned from work. For this reason alone, parents will want to give the question of plenary guardianship long and careful consideration.

If guardianship is necessary to protect your adult child and your state allows only plenary guardianship, make known your preferences for the care of your child. Speak to the guardians who will take your place, if possible, and write your preferences for care in a Letter of Intent to be attached to your will. The Letter of Intent can outline the responsibilities and objectives you hope your child will achieve. (You might for example, state your hope that your child graduate from high school.)

Limited guardian: Historically, according to most guardianship laws, judges could either declare a mentally disabled person totally incompetent and appoint a plenary guardian, or dismiss the case and leave the disabled person without the protection of a guardian. This "all or nothing" approach failed to recognize the unique needs and abilities of the disabled person, and that handicapped persons function at a variety of levels.

Most states continue to enforce such laws. However, some states now provide a less restrictive, more adaptable "limited guardianship." Some form of limited guardianship is now available in twenty-one states: Alaska, California, Colorado, Connecticut, Florida, Georgia, Hawaii, Illinois, Louisiana, Maine, Minnesota, Nevada, New Jersey, New York, Oklahoma, South Carolina, South Dakota, Texas, Vermont, Washington and Wisconsin. It is likely that many more states will pass laws to allow for limited guardianships.

A limited guardianship provides a more realistic alternative to the "all or nothing" choice between a plenary guardian or no guardian at all. Limited guardianship restricts the guardian's decision-making *only* to those decisions for which the disabled person needs help. Thus, the mentally disabled person will have responsibility over the decisions he or she is capable of making, while the guardian will be able to assist when necessary. When the disabled person lacks some, but not all, capacity to make responsible decisions, the court will appoint a limited guardian of the person, or estate, or both. In most states, unlike plenary guardianship, a limited guardianship does not constitute a finding that the disabled person is legally incompetent. The following examples will illustrate how a limited guardianship might work.

Mary is mentally retarded and forty-two years of age. Although Mary is noticeably "slow," she is very independent and stable and has worked at the local library shelving books for years. Mary also sells homemade pastries to friends and neighbors. Mary is obese and has very high blood pressure.

    After her mother's death, Mary moved in with her sister's family until they could decide on the best community facility for Mary to live in.

    They applied to a local community facility from which Mary will be able to take a bus to the library where she works. The executive director of the community facility insisted that Mary's sister become a limited guardian for Mary because of the high blood pressure. Because of Mary's independence, the limited guardian needed to have only the authority to consent to medical treatment. The executive director told the family that at the local hospital there had been increasing medical malpractice lawsuits, and most of the doctors were insisting that a guardian sign a consent-to-treatment form for mentally retarded persons because they might not have the legal mental capacity for "informed consent." Mary was admitted to the community facility after her sister became her limited guardian to consent to medical treatment. Mary retains control over the rest of the decisions in her life.

The second example illustrates a limited guardian of the estate rather than of the person:

Dick is a mentally retarded person thirty-five years of age. Dick lives in a local group home, and works in the mailing department of a local insurance company.

    When Dick's uncle died, Dick inherited $50,000. Dick's mother met with some mental health professionals and they decided Dick could competently manage his weekly salary but that he needed a limited guardian of the estate to manage and invest properly the $50,000 inheritance.

    Dick's brother, a CPA, petitions the court to be appointed a limited guardian for this purpose. The court grants the petition and Dick's brother will manage the $50,000 for the benefit of Dick. Dick can still take pride in managing his own weekly salary from the insurance company.

If the state where Dick lives allowed only the appointment of a plenary guardian, Dick's life might have been different. A plenary guardian would have total control over the $50,000 and Dick's weekly salary. Unfortunately, having lost control of his weekly salary, Dick might also have lost some of his self-esteem.

    A limited guardianship protects the disabled person without

the blanket restrictions of a plenary guardianship. It is a very flexible approach. As the above examples indicate, the range of authority granted the limited guardian can be tailored to the individual needs of the disabled individual. The appointment of a limited guardian removes from the ward only the authority which is specifically conferred on the limited guardian. Furthermore, many of the powers granted a limited guardian do not really take responsibility away from the disabled person, but allow the guardian to deal with bureaucracies on behalf of the ward (for example, to apply for and obtain funds from governmental sources for the ward, to consent to medical treatment, to examine confidential records about the disabled person). This authority for the limited guardian to represent the ward when dealing with bureaucracies is even more critical for non-related future guardians after the parent's death. The following list describes some areas in which the limited guardian might be given authority:

● To apply for and enroll the ward in

public or private residential facilities.
needed and reasonable non-residential mental retardation programs administered by public or private agencies.
educational programs.
vocational programs.

● To consent to medical and psychological tests and treatment for the ward.

● To examine, copy, redisclose confidential records.

● To attend confidential professional staff meetings.

● To apply for funds and services from governmental sources for the ward, including:

Supplemental Security Income (SSI),
Aid to Families with Dependent Children (AFDC),
Disability benefits under Social Security,
Title XX Services,
Vocational Rehabilitation Programs,
Medicaid,
Maternal and Child Health and Crippled Children's Services, and
Developmental Disability Services.

● To contract and make purchases over $_____ for the ward.

- To cancel or negate contracts and purchases made by the ward over $_____. (Note: This provision has questionable legal validity. However, it may be useful in dealing with someone who has financially exploited the ward.)

- To manage the specific properties of the ward.

- To rent or buy real estate for the ward to live in.

- To file federal or state income tax returns for the ward.

- To help the ward attain

  employment.
  an identification card.
  a driver's license.

- To file or defend a lawsuit on behalf of the ward. In establishing a limited guardianship, the family as well as the court should carefully consider the handicapped person's abilities and disabilities to insure that the proper amount of responsibility remains with the disabled person.

Successor and testamentary guardians. Two of the burning questions in the minds of parents of the disabled are "Who will care for our child after our death?" and "How can we control now the selection of a person that will have legal authority to care for our child after we are gone?" Although successor and testamentary guardianships were discussed in the wills chapter this information is so important it will be expanded on here.

A good way to provide continuity of care and security for your child is to appoint either a *successor guardian* or a *testamentary guardian*. Many states have established some form of successor or testamentary guardian.

A *successor guardian* takes the place of a guardian who can no longer perform his or her duties because of death or some other reason. *You can name a successor guardian in the court order which established the original guardianship.* When the previous guardian can no longer act as guardian, the successor guardian must notify the court and the court must approve of a successor guardian. Usually, the court is delighted to approve the successor guardian named in the original court order.

The *testamentary guardian* is a guardian named in a will rather than in the orginal guardianship order. If your state does not allow you to designate successor guardians in the court order, you should check with your lawyer to see whether or not you can name in your will a guardian to take your place. In some states, such as Illinois, only a *parent* who has been *appointed legal guardian* over his or her adult disabled child can nominate a valid testamentary guardian for the adult disabled child. For this reason alone, many parents are becoming guardians of their disabled adult children. Similar to successor guardians, the testamentary guardian must notify the court of the death of the original guardian, and the court must approve the selection of the testamentary guardian.

Normally, the successor and testamentary guardians assume the identical powers of the original guardians. Therefore, you should give the testamentary or successor guardians a copy of the guardianship order so that they will understand the exact responsibilities and authority they will have when they become guardians. The future guardians must be fully informed about the responsibilities of the appointment.

To insure that your child will have the protection of a guardian throughout his or her lifetime, try to select a successor or testamentary guardian who might be expected to live as long as your disabled child. To futher guarantee life-long guardianship protection, name more than one testamentary or successor guardian. If more than one guardian is named, be sure that you clearly indicate the order in which the guardians should assume the guardianship appointment. In choosing a successor or testamentary guardian, as in choosing all guardians, match the capabilities of the guardian with the unique needs of the disabled person.

Testamentary and successor guardianship provisions allow parents to control who will be responsible for caring for their child after their death or incapacity. If you do not nominate a future guardian, the court must select a guardian without knowing your preferences.

Private guardianship agencies. In some states a private agency, sometimes called a corporation, can be appointed as guardian of a disabled person. The laws in most of these states require that the agency be non-profit as described in section 501(c)(3) of the Internal Revenue Code of 1954.

Most of these non-profit organizations have professional staffs that can act as guardians and also advise family guardians. It is wise to inquire about staff case-loads (no more than 50 is best), frequency of visits to wards, amounts of time spent with the ward and the residential staff at each visit, size of budget, and resources.

Interview the staff to insure that they are caring rather than bureaucratic. Often, the staffs can answer questions about the local mental health network: about residential, vocational, and school placement; and about finding an attorney to draft your estate plan with your disabled child in mind. It is always worthwhile to contact these organizations to ask about their services.

If you are considering such a private agency to be named the guardian or future guardian of your adult disabled child, inquire about their budget and ask for an annual statement. You want an organization that will remain solvent during the entire lifetime of your child. Despite the expense, it is best if the organization charges for its services and is not totally reliant on government and charitable funds, which may disappear. A private, non-profit guardianship service can act quite effectively as a co-guardian or as an advisor: providing professional services and support to the disabled person and the other guardian. These organizations, if permitted by state law, can be named as co-guardians (or advisors) in a testamentary or successor guardian capacity after the parent's death.

Public guardians. If a mentally disabled person needs a guardian, but has no one to assume the responsibility, the court will appoint either a public official or a public agency such as a state-administered guardianship service to act as guardian. Often public guardians are guardians "of last resort" and provide care when

- The mentally disabled person has no relatives or friends to serve as guardian.

- No one is willing to serve as guardian.

- No one is qualified to serve as guardian.

Most public guardianship agencies have professional staffs, and do not charge for their services.

Temporary guardian. Temporary guardians (called guardians ad litem in some states) are appointed for a temporary period of time (usually, not more than 60 days) for disabled persons who do not have permanent guardians. A temporary guardian is most often used in two situations. First, a temporary guardian is appointed when urgently needed—for example, to sign a medical consent-to-treatment form for a mentally disabled adult without a permanent guardian. Second, a temporary guardian can be appointed during

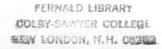

the waiting period between the filing of the petition for guardianship and the actual hearing, if there is a threat to the welfare and protection of the disabled person's estate or person.

If needed, the temporary appointment is established quickly and simply, by having a judge sign a guardianship order either with a shortened court hearing or without a court hearing. Any competent adult can be appointed a temporary guardian, and often parents themselves are appointed. The temporary guardian must meet the same qualifications of the guardian of the estate or person, but has only the authority specifically written in the court order.

If an emergency should arise in which a mentally disabled person has no appointed guardian but needs one, a temporary guardian is a feasible solution. However, even though the temporary guardian may be appointed fairly quickly, in a medical emergency the delay could be frustrating, painful, and perhaps dangerous. A permanent guardian may prevent such emergency situations.

ALTERNATIVES TO GUARDIANSHIP

Before you decide your child needs some type of guardian you should consider the alternatives to guardianship. These include trust funds, representative payees, and citizen advocates. Trust funds and representative payees are alternatives to guardians of the estate and the citizen advocate is an alternative to a guardian of the person.

Unlike guardianship, these alternatives will not provide the disabled person with a *legal* substitute decision maker. A legal substitute decision maker is more vital for caring for the personal needs of the disabled person than for financial matters. As discussed earlier, without a guardian of the person serious problems can arise such as an urgent medical situation. Substitutes to personal guardians are most appropriate for only mildly disabled persons.

Before you decide on choosing a guardian for your child or selecting an alternative, carefully consider the unique needs of your disabled child. Remember that guardianship and these "alternatives" can be combined to provide care for your child. Many parents have a guardian of the person named in order to care for the disabled individual's personal needs and establish a trust to manage the disabled person's financial affairs. This is a highly recommended approach. Similarly, families can select a personal guardian for their child and utilize the advice of mental health advocacy agencies, such as a unit of the National Association for Retarded Citizens.

Trusts. Trusts are a highly recommended alternative to a guardian of the estate. Trusts accomplish the same objective of the guardian of the estate—management of the disabled person's assets.

Trusts offer several advantages and fewer restrictions than guardians of the estate. Chief among these is a solution to the resource problems which might jeopardize the disabled person's eligibility for governmental aid (see Trusts chapter). In addition, in order to secure proper financial management it is not necessary to declare the disabled person incompetent. Nor is there a need for the constant, detailed reports that a guardian of the estate must submit to the court. It is not necessary to get approval from the court for expenditures on behalf of the disabled person. The posting of a bond is not required. (However, with a professional trustee there will be managment fees.) The trustee will also have greater flexibility in investing than a guardian of the estate.

The parents can select a trustee without the approval of the court. The trust document containing the duties of the trustee can be written to include all the preferences of the parents. The trust, like a limited guardian of the estate, can provide protection and assistance and allow the disabled person to make those financial decisions he or she is capable of making.

While family objectives will vary, normally a trust is a better alternative than a guardian of the estate. Further details about trusts may be found in chapter 3.

Representative payee. A representative payee is a person or organization authorized to cash and manage public assistance checks such as Supplementary Security Income and Social Security for a person deemed incapable of managing the money. The payee is appointed by an agency administering the funds. If the parents want a particular representative payee selected, they must notify the agency administering the funds. If the representative payee is not a relative, service fees may be required. The representative payee must keep an accurate record of all expenditures made on behalf of the disabled person. The representative payee is an alternative to a guardian of the estate if the only money the disabled person receives is from the government.

Advocacy. The family and the disabled person receive personal attention, guidance, and representation from an advocacy relationship. An advocate can be either a friend of the disabled person or a staff professional of a mental health agency. Some mental health agencies advocate or lobby for laws that will benefit disabled people as a group while other agencies lobby for *individual* disabled people and their families. These agencies that advocate for the individual can be helpful in advising the family and the disabled person concerning the services in the local area available to the disabled child. Increasingly, private, non-profit agencies are being created to provide individual advocacy support.

Although the advocate can help the disabled person on almost any matter, unlike a guardian, the advocate cannot legally make decisions for the disabled person. For instance, the advocate would be unable to contract for the disabled person, invest money without consent, or sign a medical consent-to-treatment form. Therefore, the advocate relationship is most appropriate as additional assistance to the family and the personal guardian. Advocacy can replace a personal guardian only when a commitment is formed between a caring, competent adult and a mildly disabled person.

Power of attorney. A power of attorney is a written document by which a person (the principal) authorizes another person (the agent) to act on the principal's behalf. The one holding the power of attorney is called an "attorney in fact" thus distinguishing the person from an attorney at law. The purpose of a power of attorney is to prove to a third person or organization that the agent has the authority to act on behalf of the principal. The power of attorney is a simple document to draft and can be written for almost any situation in which the attorney in fact acts on behalf of the principal—buying and selling goods, contracting with third persons, or whatever.

Technically, the distinguishing characteristic between guardianship and a power of attorney is that a guardian acts on behalf of, or in place of, a person who is to some degree *incompetent* whereas a person who has power of attorney acts on behalf of a *competent* person. A power of attorney can be an appropriate method for acting on behalf of a mildly disabled person who does not need a guardian. For instance, many parents of the disabled hold a power of attorney to fill out and submit the disabled person's taxes to the IRS. The powers of the attorney in fact are limited to those specified in the document.

HOW DO I OBTAIN A GUARDIANSHIP FOR MY CHILD?

After you have learned about the various types of guardians and have made a decision based on the needs of your disabled child, your attorney can begin legal proceedings. The proceedings will determine

- The level of competence of your child.

- The need for guardianship.

- The type of guardian to be appointed.

- The amount of authority granted the guardian.

How do I start a guardianship proceeding? To initiate the proceeding, your lawyer will file a "Petition for Appointment of Guardian for the Disabled Person" (the title of the petition may vary slightly from state to state) with the court clerk. Although each state provides a different petition form, the following information must be included by your lawyer in most petitions:

- The petitioner's relationship to and interest in the disabled person. The petitioner is the person who asks the court to appoint a guardian for the disabled person.

- The name, date of birth, and place of residence of the disabled person.

- The reasons for requesting a guardianship.

- The name and address of the proposed guardian, and, if an individual, his or her age and occupation.

- The approximate value of the disabled person's personal property and real estate.

- The approximate amount of the disabled person's gross annual income and other receipts.

- The names and addresses of the nearest relatives of the disabled person.

Notice to the disabled person. A formal notice or "summons" is then given to the disabled person to show that a guardianship petition has been filed. The summons indicates the time, date, and location of the court hearing. In most states, a summons and copy of the petition must be delivered or "served" on the alleged disabled person not less than 14 days before the hearing.

In some states, the sheriff delivers the summons to the disabled person. As a parent, if you believe a sheriff, who is a stranger, would frighten your child, ask your lawyer to motion the court for permission to use a "special process server." The special process server is a person other than the sheriff who will deliver the summons to your child. With the approval of the court, the special process server in most states can be anybody over the age of eighteen who is not a party to the guardianship case. Therefore, with court permission you can select a friend of the family to deliver the summons.

Evidence of incapacity. In most states, attached to the Petition for Guardianship there must be a report by a physician. This physician is often a psychiatrist or an expert who has experience with the particular disability involved, and must have examined the disabled person usually within 90 days of the hearing. The judge reads the physician's report as evidence of the mental capacity of the disabled person, in order to establish the need for guardianship and as an aid in determining the type and powers of the guardian. The psychiatrist must fill out a form usually containing the following information:

● Description of the nature and type of disability.

● Evaluation of the disabled person's mental and physical condition including educational level, adaptive behavior, and social skills.

● An opinion of whether a guardian is needed.

● An opinion, with reasons, as to the type and scope of guardianship needed.

● A recommendation, with reasons, as to the most suitable living arrangement and, where appropriate, treatment, and rehabilitation plan.

● The signatures of all persons who performed the evaluations on which the report is based. At least one of these persons must be a licensed physician.

You should ask your lawyer for the physician's report form, have a doctor fill it out, then show it to your attorney. Your lawyer, after reading the report, will be able to determine how likely the judge will be to grant the guardianship. By determining the potential of the case prior to the court hearing, you can save considerable time and expense that might otherwise be wasted. Normally, a guardianship case will cost between $100 and $500, including legal fees and court costs.

In order to justify the need for a guardian, the doctor's report must clearly and accurately demonstrate that the handicapped person's disability creates a need for guardianship. The doctor's report must not be vague. For instance, if the physician's report states only "This person in mentally ill and needs a guardian," this will not be a sufficient description to justify to the court the need for guardianship.

The same report written more specifically could probably justify the need for a guardian. Rather than just stating "this person is mentally ill and needs a guardian," the doctor might write:

This person has had learning and emotional problems, probably related to unknown organic damage. He has had several schizo-affective psychotic episodes in which he was violent toward others. He will require psychiatric supervision, counseling, and psychotropic medication (currently Navone and Lithium). With Navone and Lithium he is free of psychotic symptoms. But he is incapable of independent living or of work because of an inability to make independent judgments in regard to personal care and ordinary social life.

He is in need of a limited guardian of the person. He needs assistance in making personal, financial, and medical decisions. He is capable of making daily decisions of personal care within a stable, protected, non-challenging environment. He will need guardianship authority to make decisions about residential placement through his lifetime. He also needs medication for heart problems and may need hospitalization in the future. (Note: If your child does need help in making decisions in regard to residential placement it is wise to have the doctor comment on this. Most judges are understandably reluctant to give this authority to the guardian unless absolutely necessary.)

or

Miss Doe has borderline mental retardation with intellectual scores in the 60 to 70 range. She is working at the Work Center—a sheltered workshop. Miss Doe is partially incapable of making personal and financial decisions. I do believe she is entirely incapable of handling financial affairs. She also needs help in making decisions in regard to her health.

Most states require at least one of the persons who performed the evaluation to testify at the hearing, unless excused by the court.

Appointment of a Guardian Ad Litem. A guardian ad litem (GAL) is a person appointed by the court to represent a mentally disabled person for the purpose and duration of a legal proceeding without having guardianship control over the disabled individual's person or estate. The GAL serves to protect the interests of the disabled person usually during the guardianship proceedings.

A GAL, when appointed, examines the case and determines the rights of the disabled person and defends him or her if necessary. For purposes of a guardianship proceeding, the GAL is often an attorney appointed by the court to visit the alleged disabled person and write a report for the court indicating whether or not a guardian is needed, and, if so, what type of guardian should be appointed with what powers to protect the interests and insure the welfare of the disabled person.

Acting as a investigator, the GAL visits the alleged disabled person in his or her normal living environment. If it is a residential facility, the GAL also meets with the staff and discusses the long-term prognosis for the disabled person. The GAL must inform the disabled person (often, orally and in writing) of the guardianship proceeding, the contents of the petition for guardianship, and the various procedural rights available to the disabled person.

In the report to the court the GAL will discuss the alleged disabled person's medical records, functional level, and long-term prognosis. The GAL will indicate to the court whether the disabled person will need the help of a guardian in personal and/or financial matters. If, in the opinion of the GAL, a guardian is needed, he or she will also recommend the type of guardian that would seem to be most appropriate. The GAL might communicate to the court the disabled person's preference for a particular individual to be appointed guardian.

In many states, one must pay a GAL (approximately $100 to $400) for his or her services. If you cannot afford a GAL, in some states the court will enter an order on the state to pay the GAL fees. Moreover, in some states the judge may waive the requirement of a GAL and thus substantially reduce costs. If state laws permit such a waiver, the judge will most likely waive the requirement for a GAL when a close family member seeks guardianship and the medical report on the disabled person appears conclusive and accurate. Sometimes the judge will agree to visit with the disabled person in his or her chambers rather than appoint a GAL. To avoid the cost of a GAL, ask your lawyer whether the laws in your state and the circumstances of the case warrant a waiver of a GAL.

Hearing and appointment. Usually, the actual guardianship hearing can be completed in about a half hour or less. It is the pre-hearing documentation that takes the time. The judge will examine the petition for guardianship, the physician's report, and any other documents. Your lawyer will explain the need for and type of guardian requested and answer any questions by the judge. The judge will talk with the disabled person.

If the judge believes the evidence justifies the need to appoint a guardian, he or she will sign a court order appointing the guardian. Remember, the guardian's powers are *restricted* to those granted by the court. The guardianship order will specify the exact responsibilities and powers the guardian will assume.

Additionally, a case number will be on the guardianship order. The case number identifies the court case. If a question arises in the future, the guardian can give the case number to a court clerk who can look up the case for clarification.

The formal document issued by the court indicating the appointment of a guardian is usually called the "Letters of Office." The guardian can use this document to prove guardianship.

After the guardian has been appointed by the court, the guardian should notify the disabled ward's contacts such as hospitals, stores, relatives. These people and institutions should be informed who the ward's guardian is so they can contact him or her if they become aware of any problems. Also, this notification might protect the ward from someone's unscrupulous actions.

Modification or discharge of guardianship. By petitioning the court, the ward, the guardian, or any interested person can seek a change of termination in the guardianship. A hearing on the petition is required. If you want to change the authority the guardian has, the petition must list the reasons for seeking the modification. Most modifications involve a change in a guardian or an alteration in the guardian's authority—decreasing or increasing it.

Usually a guardian continues until he or she is granted permission to resign. However, a guardianship will terminate if

- The ward no longer needs a guardian.

- The guardian is no longer willing or able to continue.

- The guardian does not do a competent job.

- The guardian is convicted of a felony.

- The guardian wastes or mismanages the ward's estate.

- The guardian fails to file an inventory and accounting after being ordered to do so.

- The guardian becomes a nonresident of the state.

- The ward dies.

Rights of the disabled person. The laws in all states entitle the disabled person to rights at the guardianship hearing to insure a guardian is not appointed when a less restrictive alternative would be sufficient to insure that the proper type of guardian is appointed. Most states entitle the alleged disabled person to

- Be represented by an attorney.

- Demand a jury trial.

- Be present at the hearing.

- Have the hearing closed to the public.

- Present evidence.

- Confront and cross-examine witnesses.

- Be examined independently by one or more doctors.

In most instances, these rights are not called upon because a parent or a concerned person is properly being appointed guardian. However, these rights provide a safeguard against exploitation.

Checklist of procedures for your lawyer. (Note: Each state will vary slightly in procedure.)

- Obtain evidence of incapacity of the disabled person to be submitted at the guardianship hearing. The physician's report should be filled out in detail. (See page 44.)[1]

- Prepare a petition for guardianship and file it with the court clerk. (See page 45.)

- Prepare summons to be served on the disabled person. Obtain hearing date and place from the court clerk and give the summons to the sheriff for service. Or prepare an order to use a special process server and an affidavit. (See pages 46, 47, and 48.)

[1](Note: Since guardianship forms vary from state to state, the following forms are included only as illustrations of the type of information required. These examples are based on those used by the Circuit Court of Cook County, Illinois.)

• Prepare a court order appointing a guardian ad litem (GAL); or prepare an order to waive the GAL. (See page 49.)

• Prepare the mailing of notice to relatives and other persons named in the petition.

• If necessary, prepare a petition and order for a temporary guardian. (See pages 50 and 51.)

• Prepare a court order waiving the presence of the disabled person or the physician if either cannot attend the hearing.

• Prepare a court order appointing a plenary or limited guardian. (See pages 52 and 53.)

• Prepare an oath and bond of representative to submit to the court. (See pages 54 and 55.)

• If necessary, prepare a petition and order to deposit the ward's funds in an account. (See pages 56 and 57.)

• If necessary, prepare a petition and order for authority to make expenditures on behalf of the ward. (See pages 58 and 59.)

CONCLUSION

The first step in deciding whether a guardian is necessary is to analyze the capabilities and needs of your disabled child. How vulnerable is your child? Can your child make personal and financial decisions? Would less restrictive alternatives such as social services and trusts be sufficient?

If a guardian is needed, have a physician write a detailed medical report on your child. Remember this report will be attached to the Petition for Guardianship. Determine the type of guardian to be requested—personal or estate, or both, plenary or limited.

If possible, name a successor guardian in the guardianship order. If no successor guardian has been named in the order, if possible nominate a testamentary guardian in your will.

After the judge appoints a guardian, look at the court order which specifies the authority of the guardian. Find out how often and in what detail the guardian must report to the court.

If you have taken all these precautions and have provided a sensitive and knowledgeable guardian for your child, you can feel confident that you have done your best for your child's future.

44

REPORT

ESTATE OF

No. _____

Docket _____

Alleged Disabled Person   Page _____

REPORT

_____ , a physician licensed to practice medicine in all its branches, submits the following report on _____ alleged disabled person, based on an examination of the respondent on _____ , 19 _____

1. Describe the nature and type of the respondent's disability:

2. Describe the respondent's mental and physical condition and, where appropriate, describe educational condition, adaptive behavior, and social skills.

3. State whether, in your opinion, the respondent is totally or only partially incapable of making personal and financial decisions, and if the latter, the kinds of decisions which the respondent can and cannot make. Include the response for this opinion.

4. What, in your opinion, is the most appropriate living arrangement for the respondent, and if applicable, describe the most appropriate treatment or habilitation plan. Include the reasons for your opinion.

Signed: * _____

Address _____

City and State _____

Telephone _____

* This report must be signed by a physician. If the description of the respondent's mental, physical and educational condition, adaptive behavior or social skills is based on evaluations by other professionals, all professionals preparing evaluations must also sign the report. Evaluations on which the report is based must have been performed within 3 months of the date of the filing of the petition.

Names and signatures of other persons who performed evaluations upon which this report is based:

Name _____

Address _____

Signature _____

Name _____

Address _____

Signature _____

**Petition For Appointment of Guardian
For Disabled Person**   **(7-81) CCP-200**

Estate of

} No.

Docket

Alleged Disabled Person } Page

Hearing on petition
set for

_____, 19___

_____, on oath states:

1. _____, whose date of birth is_____ and
place of residence is _____, is a disabled person.

2. The relationship to and interest of the petitioner in the respondent is:

_____

3. The reason for the guardianship is that the respondent is a disabled person due to:

_____

and because of such disability* (a) lacks sufficient understanding or capacity to make or communicate responsible decisions concerning the care of the respondent's person; (b) is unable to manage the respondent's estate or financial affairs.

4. a. The approximate value of estate:

Personal_____Real _____

b. The anticipated gross annual income and other receipts of the respondent are $_____

5. The names and post-office addresses of the respondent's nearest relatives and guardian, if any, are listed on Exhibit A attached hereto and made a part of this petition. (List spouse and adult children; if none, the respondent's parents and adult brothers and sisters; if none, nearest kindred.)

6. The name and address of the person with whom, or the facility in which the respondent is residing is:

_____

Petitioner asks that: (a)_____be adjudged a disabled person;

(b) _____
         (name)   (address)

_____age_____years,_____
    (city and state)   (occupation)

qualified and willing to act; be appointed as guardian of the

Respondent's _____
      (estate)   (estate and person)

(c) _____
    (name)   (address)

_____age_____years,_____
    (city and state)   (occupation)

qualified to act, be appointed as guardian of the person only.

Name
Attorney for Petitioner   **Petitioner**
Address
City   Address_____
Telephone
                       City_____

* Strike if not applicable.

Signed and sworn to before me this day of_____, 19___

_____ Notary public

Summons For Appointment of Guardian For Disabled Person
(10-81) CCP-201

Estate of

Alleged Disabled Person

No.

Docket

Page

SUMMONS FOR APPOINTMENT OF GUARDIAN FOR DISABLED PERSON

To

You are summoned to appear at a hearing on a petition to adjudge you a disabled person and have a guardian appointed to make decisions for you regarding yourself or your property or both. A copy of the petition is attached.

On _____ , 19___ at ___ a.m./p.m., a hearing will be held at Room ___ to determine whether or not a guardian shall be appointed for you.

At the hearing, you have a right to be represented by a lawyer. You have the right to attend the hearing. If you do not have a lawyer, the court will appoint one for you upon your written or oral request communicated to the court prior to or at the hearing. You have the right to demand a jury trial. You may confront and cross-examine all witnesses and present your own witnesses. You have the right to request that your hearing be closed to the public. You have the right to request that an expert be appointed to examine you.

TO THE OFFICER:

This summons must be served on the alleged disabled person personally not later than 14 days before the day for appearance. The summons must be returned by the officer, or other person to whom it was given for service, with endorsement of service and fees, if any, not later than 2 days after service. If service cannot be made on the alleged disabled person personally, this summons shall be returned so endorsed.

Witness _____ , 19___

_____
Clerk of Court
(Seal of Court)

RETURN

I certify that on _____ , 19___ , I served this summons on the alleged disabled person by leaving a copy with him/her personally and informing him/her of its contents.

_____ Sheriff of ___ County

By _____ Deputy

SHERIFF'S FEES

Name

Attorney for Petitioner

Address

City

Telephone

Service and return ___ $ ___

Miles ___ $ ___

Total ___ $ ___

CCG-2   **ORDER**

COUNTY   PROBATE

_____ DEPARTMENT _____

(COUNTY) (MUNICIPAL)   (DIVISION) (DISTRICT)

Estate of:

_____ } NO. _____

Doc. _____

Page _____

ORDER

On the motion of _____, attorney
for the Petitioner;

It is hereby ordered that John Doe, a private person
over the age of eighteen (18), and not a party to
the above captioned cause, is authorized and directed
to serve the process of this Honorable Court on
_____, the Respondent in this cause.

48

Affidavit of Special Process Server   CCG-60 (8-80)

_____ DEPARTMENT_____
(County)   (Municipal)   (Division)   (District)

No. _____

_____

being first duly sworn on oath deposes and says that he was appointed by the Court on

_____, 19_____to serve process in the above mentioned cause.

I. That he served the within summons and a copy of the complaint on the within

named defendant, _____

by leaving a copy of each with the said defendant personally

on_____, 19____

II. That he served the within summons and a copy of the complaint on the within

named defendant, _____

by leaving a copy of each at his usual place of abode with _____

_____ a person of the family of the age of

13 years or upwards and informed that person of the contents thereof

on _____, 19____

III.   (a) That the sex, race and approximate age of the defendant or other person

with whom he left the summons are as follows:

Sex _____Race_____Approximate Age _____

(b) That the place where (if possible in terms of an exact street address) and

the date and time of the day when the summons was left with the defendant or

other person were as follows:

Place, _____

Date, _____Time of the day, _____

IV. That he was unable to serve the within named defendant.

_____

SPECIAL PROCESS SERVER (signature)

Signed and sworn to before me_____

_____, 19____

_____

Notary public

Order Appointing Guardian Ad Litem
For Alleged Disabled Person   **(11-81) CCP-209**

ESTATE OF

}

No. _____

Docket _____

Alleged Disabled Person   Page _____

ORDER APPOINTING GUARDIAN AD LITEM FOR

ALLEGED DISABLED PERSON

Pursuant to the provisions of Sec. 11a-10 of the Probate Act, _____

_____ is appointed

guardian ad litem and counsel * for the above named respondent.

The guardian ad litem is directed to personally interview the respondent and inform respondent orally and in writing of the contents of the petition and of a respondent's rights under Sec. 11a-11 of the Probate Act.

The guardian ad litem is further directed to file a written report with the

Court and to be present at the hearing in Room _____,

on _____, 19____ at _____ .M.

_____, 19_____

ENTER:

_____

                      Judge

Name
Attorney for Petitioner
Address
City
Telephone

*Strike if not applicable.

**Petition for Temporary Guardian
for Disabled Person**   **(6-81) CCP-202**

Estate of   NO.

       }   Docket

Alleged Disabled Person   Page

PETITION FOR TEMPORARY GUARDIAN

_____, on oath states:

1. On _____ , 19____, a petition was filed herein for the appointment of a

guardian of the _____
           (Estate and Person)   (Estate)   (Person)

of _____

2. A temporary guardian is necessary for the welfare and protection of the respondent

because:

Petitioner ask that _____
          (Name)   (Address)

_____ years.
      (City and State)   (Age)

_____, qualified and willing to act, be appointed as
     (Occupation)

temporary guardian of the _____
          (Estate and Person)   (Estate)   (Person)

_____ of the alleged disabled person.

Name   _____
Attorney for   (Petitioner)
Address
City   _____
Telephone   (Address)

                     _____
                   (City and State)

Signed and sworn to before me _____, 19 ____

                     _____
           (Clerk of Court)   (Notary Public)

ORDER APPOINTING TEMPORARY GUARDIAN
FOR DISABLED PERSON   CCP-203

ESTATE OF

} No. _____

    Docket _____

Alleged Disabled Person   Page _____

ORDER APPOINTING TEMPORARY GUARDIAN

On the petition of _____

for appointment of a temporary guardian, the court having found that the appointment

is necessary for the welfare and protection of the alleged disabled person or his estate.

It is ordered that _____ is appointed

temporary guardian for the respondent's _____
                     (Estate and Person)   (Estate)   (Person)

_____ and that letters of temporary guardianship

issue.

The powers and duties of the temporary guardian are as follows:

_____, 19_____

ENTER:

Name   _____

Attorney for Petitioner   Judge

Address

City

Telephone

(3-81) CCP-204

ESTATE OF   } No.

                Docket

     A Disabled Person   Page

ORDER APPOINTING PLENARY GUARDIAN FOR A DISABLED PERSON

On the verified petition of _____ for an adjudication

of disability and the appointment of a guardian for the _____
                                                              (estate and person)

_____ of the above named disabled person, the Court,
(estate)   (person)

having heard the evidence presented, finds:

     1. That respondent is a disabled person and is*
         (a) totally without understanding or capacity to make or communicate
             decisions regarding his/her person:
         (b) totally unable to manager his/her estate or financial affairs.

     2. The factual basis for the findings of the Court is as follows:

_____

_____

_____

_____

_____

IT IS ORDERED THAT:

A. _____ is appointed plenary

     guardian of the _____ of the disabled person.
                         (estate)   (estate and person)

B. _____ is appointed plenary

     guardian of the person of the disabled person.

C. The duration and term of the plenary guardianship shall be _____

D. No/An authorization to appraise goods and chattels issue.

E. Letters of plenary guardianship shall issue in accordance with the provisions

of this order.

Name   _____, 19____

Attorney for Petitioner

Address   ENTER:

City

Telephone   _____
                                    Judge

*Strike (a) or (b) if not applicable.

(6-81) CCP-207

ESTATE OF

No.

Docket

Disabled Person } Page

ORDER APPOINTING LIMITED GUARDIAN FOR DISABLED PERSON

On the verified petition of _____

for an adjudication of disability and the appointment of a guardian for the

_____ of the above

(estate and person) (estate) (person)

named disabled person, the Court, having heard the evidence presented, finds:

1. That respondent is a disabled person and*
   (a) lacks some but not all the understanding or capacity to make or communicate responsible decisions concerning the care of respondent's person;
   (b) lacks some but not all of the ability to manage respondent's estate or financial affairs.
2. The factual basis for the finding of the Court is as follows:

_____

_____

_____

IT IS HEREBY ORDERED THAT:

A. _____ is appointed limited

guardian of the _____ of the disabled person.
                 (estate)   (estate and person)

B. _____ is appointed limited

guardian of the person of the disabled person.

C. The limits of the duties and powers of the guardian(s) are as follows: _____

_____

_____

_____

D. The legal disabilities to which the disabled person is subject are as follows: ____

_____

_____

_____

E. Letters of limited guardianship shall issue in accordance with the provision of this order.

_____, 19____

Name   ENTER:
Attorney for Petitioner
Address
City   _____
Telephone   Judge
*Strike (a) or (b) if not applicable.

OATH AND BOND OF REPRESENTATIVE - NO SURETY

CCP-313 (12-79)

Estate of

No.

} Docket

Page

OATH AND BOND OF REPRESENTATIVE - NO SURETY

I, _____, on oath state that I

will discharge faithfully the duties of the office of representative, and I bind

myself to the People of the State of _____

to the faithful discharge of those duties.

The obligation of this bond is limited to $_____

APPROVED: _____

_____, 19____   Address _____

_____   City _____
                Judge

Name   Signed and sworn to before me

Attorney for   _____, 19____

Address   _____
                                         (Clerk of Court) (Notary public)

City

Telephone

*First name of representative must be written in full.

OATH AND BOND OF REPRESENTATIVE - SURETY

(5-79) CCP-312

Estate of

} No.

Docket

Page

OATH AND BOND OF REPRESENTATIVE - SURETY

I, _____, on oath state that I will faithfully discharge the duties of the office of representative. I and the undersigned sureties jointly and severally bind ourselves to the People of the State of _____ to the faithful discharge of those duties.

The obligation of this bond is limited to $_____

APPROVED

_____, 19____

_____
Judge

*_____
as representative and principal

Address _____

City _____

*_____
as surety

Address _____

City _____

*_____
as surety

Address _____

City _____

Signed and sworn to before me by the representative on

_____, 19____

_____
(Clerk of Court) (Notary Public)

Name
Attorney for
Address
City
Telephone

*First name of each principal and individual surety must be written in full.

PETITION TO DEPOSIT FUNDS SUBJECT TO FURTHER ORDER OF COURT

In the Matter of the Estate)
)   File No.
         of   )   Docket
)   Page
_____, a Disabled Person)

PETITION

Your petitioner, _____ respectfully states:
                    (Guardian)

1. He was duly appointed Guardian of the Estate of _____ a Disabled Person by this court on _____, 19_____.

2. The assets of the estate consist of cash in the amount of _____ dollars; that no additional assets or benefits are due or payable to the ward or his estate.

3. He believes it is in the best interests of the ward and his estate to deposit the balance of cash on hand in the amount of _____ dollars, in the _____Bank, in the name of the ward, subject to further order of this court, and to close the estate.

WHEREFORE, petitioner prays that he be authorized to deposit the balance of cash in his possession in the amount of _____ dollars in the _____ Bank in the name of the ward, subject to further order of the Court and to close the estate.

_____
                  GUARDIAN

State of Illinois   )
)   SS.
County of _____)

_____, being first duly sworn, on oath says that he has read the foregoing Petition by him subscribed, knows the contents thereof, and that the statements therein are true.

_____

ORDER TO DEPOSIT FUNDS SUBJECT TO FURTHER ORDER OF COURT

In the Matter of the Estate   )
)   File No.
       of   )   Docket
)   Page
_____, a Disabled Person   )

ORDER

This cause coming on to be heard (with or without notice) on the verified petition of _____, Guardian of the Estate of _____, a Disabled Person for leave to deposit funds of the ward subject to further order of this court, and the court having considered the petition and being fully advised in the premises, finds:

That the assets of the estate consist of cash in the amount of _____ dollars, and that no additional assets or benefits are due or payable to the ward or his estate;

That it is in the best interests of the ward and his estate to deposit the balance of cash in possession of the guardian, in the amount of _____ dollars, in the _____ Bank, in the name of the ward, subject to further order of this court, and to close the estate.

IT IS THEREFORE ORDERED that _____, Guardian of the Estate of _____, a Disabled Person be and he hereby is authorized and directed to deposit the balance of cash in his possession in the amount of _____ dollars, in the _____ Bank in the name of the ward, _____, subject to further order of this court, and to close the estate.

_____, 19_____

ENTER:_____

PETITION FOR AUTHORITY TO MAKE EXPENDITURES

In the Matter of the Estate   )
)   File No.
            of   )   Docket
)   Page
_____, a Disabled Person   )

PETITION

Your petition, _____, respectfully states:
              (Guardian)

1. He was duly appointed Guardian of the Estate of _____, a Disabled Person by this court on _____, 19_____.

2. The assets of the estate consist of cash in the amount of _____ dollars, together with (OASI, VA or Civil Service) benefits in the amount of _____ dollars per month.

3. The ward is a patient at _____ (nursing home or hospital) at _____, in _____, and is in need of _____ dollars per month for care and maintenance, _____ dollars per month for incidental personal expenses, and a sum not to exceed _____ dollars per year for clothing, medical and other special expenses.

4. No previous order authorizing expenditures has been entered herein. (Or, The previous order entered herein on _____, 19_____, authorized expenditure of _____ dollars per month for care and maintenance and a further sum not to exceed _____ dollars per year for clothing, medical and other special expenses until further order of court.)

WHEREFORE, petitioner prays that he be authorized to expend the sum of _____ dollars per month for the care and maintenance of the ward, _____ dollars per month for incidental personal expenses, and a sum not to exceed _____ dollars per year for clothing, medical and other special expenses, until further order of this court.

                                                      _____
                                                          GUARDIAN

ORDER FOR EXPENDITURES

In the Matter of the Estate   )
)   File No.
        of   )   Docket
)   Page
_____, a Disabled Person   )

ORDER

This cause coming on to be heard (with or without notice) on the verified petition of _____ , Guardian of the Estate of _____, a Disabled Person, for leave to expend funds of his ward, and the court having considered the petition and being fully advised in the premises, finds:

That the ward is a patient at _____, at _____, in _____, and is in need of _____ dollars per month for care and maintenance, _____ dollars per month for incidental personal expenses, and a sum not to exceed _____ dollars per year for clothing, medical and other special expenses;

That no previous order authorizing expenditures has been entered herein. (Or, The previous order entered herein on _____ authorized, etc.)

IT IS THEREFORE ORDERED that _____, Guardian of the Estate of _____, a Disabled Person, be and he hereby is authorized and directed to expend the sum of _____ dollars per month for the ward's care and maintenance, _____ dollars per month for incidental personal expenses, and a sum not to exceed _____ dollars per year for clothing, medical, and other special expenses, until further order of this court.

_____, 19_____

ENTER:

_____
JUDGE

Chapter 3
Trusts

The trust is the most useful estate planning tool available for providing future financial security for mentally disabled persons. The trust can accomplish many estate planning goals. For example, a trust can

• Through a trustee, manage the money for a mentally disabled person by investing it properly, conserving the assets of the trust over the entire lifetime of the person, paying bills, and contracting for care. This money management is one of the most beneficial features of a trust whether or not the family sets up the trust with government benefits in mind.

• Be used by the parents of the disabled child to control the distribution of their property not only after their deaths, but also after the death of their disabled child.

• Be extremely flexible yet very specific in providing for the particular needs of the disabled person.

• Reduce taxes by shifting income producing assets from the parents who are usually in a higher tax bracket to a disabled child who is most likely in a lower tax bracket. As will be discussed later, this advantage primarily depends upon whether or not the assets in trust were irrevocably placed into the trust.

• Allow the trust property to bypass the probate proceedings which are often lengthy and costly.

• Avoid the problems of direct inheritance that may render the disabled person ineligible for government benefits by giving legal title or ownership of the assets to the trustee.

● Avoid the problems of direct inheritance that expose the disabled person's assets to collection by government creditors who provide services to the mentally disabled person.

These last two items are especially important. As you recall, if parents give money or cash-like assets to their disabled child by gift or by will many serious problems occur. First, the mentally disabled child may be incapable of wisely managing the money. Second, the gift or bequest by will might jeopardize the disabled person's eligibility for government benefits. Third, in many states the government will seize the disabled person's assets for reimbursement for mental health services rendered to him or her. In other words, if your disabled child receives money by way of gift or inheritance this money might go directly to the state, leaving your child worse off. A trust may avoid this pointless evaporation of funds. It can give parents the ability to indirectly provide their disabled child with some resources in addition to the benefits received from the government.

WHAT IS A TRUST?

Property in *trust* is held, managed, and owned by a person or institution (the trustee) for the benefit of those persons or organizations for whom the trust was created (the beneficiary). The person who places assets into the trust is commonly referred to as the creator, settlor, grantor, or trustor. The trust is a legal instrument that separates the responsibility of ownership of specific property from the benefit of ownership. The person who has responsibility of ownership is called the trustee. The trustee manages the assets according to the instructions written in the trust agreement by the creator of the trust. The trustee manages the trust property *only* for the benefit of the beneficiary. The trustee derives no benefit from the trust property except the compensation he or she may receive for performing his or her duties. The person who has the benefit of ownership is called the beneficiary. The property placed into the trust is divided into principal and income. The principal is the property that has been placed into trust and it generates income.

In a typical case, Grandfather Jones gives the bank 10,000 shares of Widget Company stock. The bank agrees to hold the stock in trust for the benefit of his son, Mr. Jones, and for Mr. Jones' two children. The *trust agreement* states that the bank will give Mr. Jones for life all the dividends accrued from the stock (the stock income). After Mr. Jones' death, the stock will be given to Mr. Jones' children and the trust will end.

Grandfather Jones is the *creator,* the person who places the property into a trust. The bank is the *trustee* and has legal ownership of the stock which is the *trust principal.* Therefore, the bank can vote the shares of stock. However, the bank holds the stock for the benefit of Mr. Jones and his two children. The bank, as trustee, has the duty of managing the stock or trust property according to the wishes of the creator, Grandfather Jones, as expressed in the trust agreement.

Mr. Jones and his two children are the *beneficiaries* of the trust. Mr. Jones is a *life tenant* because he has the right to receive income from the stock for his entire lifetime. His children are *remaindermen,* because they have a remainder interest in receiving the trust property when the life estate ends.

GRANDFATHER JONES
(Creator or Grantor)

TRUSTEE
(Could be an individual instead of a bank)

Trustee owns the
stock and can vote
the shares
(the principal)

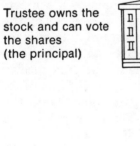

MR. JONES
(Life Tenant)

MR. JONES' CHILDREN
(Remaindermen)

Receive the trust property when life estate ends

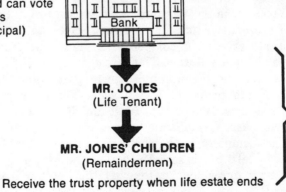

Beneficiaries

TRUSTS FOR MENTALLY DISABLED BENEFICIARIES

Trusts for healthy beneficiaries are generally used to provide income for the education or support of the beneficiaries until they reach an age when they can manage the money themselves. Trusts for mentally disabled beneficiaries, who may have no means of support after their parents die, need a trustee to manage their money for their entire lifetime. Most families do not have enough assets to put into a trust to generate approximately $30,000 a year income to provide for the current yearly costs of private care for the mentally disabled beneficiary. Therefore, the family must rely on governmental aid. However, when a disabled person is beneficiary to a trust and receives governmental aid two problems can result. The state can attempt to seize the trust property for services rendered to the disabled beneficiary and/or it can count the trust income and principal when determining the disabled person's eligibility for governmental aid.

Generally, in determining a disabled person's financial eligibility for various government benefits, assets held in a trust cannot be considered because legal ownership rests with the trustee. Therefore, if parents put money and cash-like assets into a trust for the benefit of their children rather than using a gift or a will, the children will have the benefit of the money *and* remain eligible for government benefits. However, this advantage is possible only if the trust is set up in particular ways. *Not just any trust will do!*

What distinguishes one trust from another is the variation in the powers and duties of the trustee and the purpose for which the trust was drafted. *Very specific limitations* must be placed on the powers of the trustee and the purpose of the trust must be stated very carefully. According to recent cases in many states, if the trustee has broad discretionary powers over the expenditure of the trust property for the care of the disabled beneficiary, the trust income and principal may be exposed to collection by the government for services rendered to the disabled person. It can collect for services such as out-patient care, at-home care, residential care, or any other form of government assistance that has been or is being provided. Why? The courts reason that because the trustee has the power and duty to care for the general welfare of the disabled person, the trustee's powers and the trust's purposes are identical with the state's goals to care for the general welfare of mentally disabled people. Since the state is helping fulfill the purpose of the trust, the state may charge the trust for current and past services rendered. In fact, some states argue that it is thus onforcing the rights of the disabled beneficiary!

Many states also argue from a policy standpoint that they must be allowed to seek payment from those recipients who can "afford" to pay in order to lessen the burden on other taxpayers. These states do not want to maintain a public charity for those who can "afford" to pay for their services. Depending on the particular state program, it is often against public policy to provide aid for someone who has more than $1,500 in available assets, even though $1,500 is far from enough to afford necessary services.

CREATING A TRUST

• Be wary of using standardized trust forms. The trust forms bought from the neighborhood stationery store will not address the special concerns of the mentally disabled. Also, be wary of the lawyer who uses the same trust for a healthy beneficiary as he or she does for a disabled beneficiary. Drastic results might occur, particularly in the area of government benefits.

• The trust language should explicitly state the purpose for which the trust was drafted. Often this statement of the purpose of the trust gives guidance to the trustee and to the courts if the trust is challenged. For example:

This trust is intended primarily for the benefit of my mentally disabled son Dan Smith and only incidentally for the benefit of the other beneficiaries, John Smith and Mary Smith.

or

This trust is intended to insure that there will always be an advocate to protect the legal rights of my mentally disabled daughter Mary Jones, the beneficiary, and that Mary Jones will receive the necessary assistance to achieve a reasonable degree of normal life and happiness.

As mentioned earlier, some courts are allowing the state to be reimbursed from the trust property for the costs of providing services to the mentally disabled person. To avoid this, the purpose statement of the trust is essential. A trust whose purpose is to "supplement" government aid will protect the trust property from government creditors better than a trust purpose which provides for the "general care, comfort, and welfare" of the mentally disabled beneficiary. For example

*The express purpose of this trust is to provide for John Doe's extra and
supplemental needs, over and above the benefits John otherwise receives as a
result of his handicap or disability from any local, state, or federal
government or from private agencies, any of which provide services or
benefits to disabled persons. Anything to the contrary herein
notwithstanding, no trust income or principal shall be paid to or expended
for the benefit of John so long as there are sufficient monies available to
him for his care, comfort, and welfare from federal, state, and local
government agencies and departments. The trustee shall consider such
governmental funds in determining whether there are funds available to the
beneficiary from sources other than the trust estate and shall use trust
assets only to supplement and never to substitute for such funds. In no event
may trust income or principal be paid to or for the benefit of a
governmental agency or department, and the trust estate shall at all times be
free of the claims of such governmental bodies.*

This trust purpose is different from the general "care and support"
or "discretionary" trust because the trust expressly limits the
trustee to providing only funds needed in excess of those supplied
by government agencies. It should be noted that this type of trust
should be upheld by courts as long as the courts continue to
consider the intention of the creator or the purpose of the trust to be
paramount. From reading the law, the reasonable interpretation is
that this trust will be upheld in a court of law. Lawyers who
specialize in writing these trusts agree this is the best approach
even though this exact language has not been tested in the courts.
Consult with your attorney to check the status of these laws in your
state. In the back of this chapter are various articles and cases to
further inform your attorney and save you time and expense.

Another alternative or addition to the "supplemental benefits"
purpose is to add language specifying that the trustee can pay only
for *specific* goods and services. Again, these goods and services
cannot duplicate those goods and services provided by the government. For example

*This trust is established for the benefit of my handicapped son, John Doe.
The trustee shall distribute the funds of the trust to pay only for luxuries
over and above the benefits John otherwise receives as a result of his
disability from any local, state, or federal government or from private
agencies, any of which provide services or benefits to disabled persons.
These luxuries include travel expenses to visit friends and relatives,
household furniture and appliances, clothing, movies, a record player . . .*

As you can see, the purpose of the trust should be individually
tailored to your objectives, and, therefore, a standard trust obtained

from a stationery store, a law book, or a lawyer's word processing machine will be insufficient.

● The trustee should be prohibited from distributing substantial amounts of cash assets to the disabled individual because they will create the problems outlined earlier. Governmental benefits may be reduced or lost even in cases where the cash was given as a "supplemental benefit." In such cases, the trustee should be instructed to purchase only *goods* and *services* for the mentally disabled beneficiary. And, the trustee rather than directly distribute money to the disabled person should be restricted to purchasing only those goods and services which are not available free from the government. For example, the trustee should not pay for residential living for the beneficiary if the government provides many types of residential alternatives for disabled persons.

● Give the trustee as much discretion as possible over the management and expenditure of the trust principal and income. Unlike a guardian of the estate, who may be hampered by conservative investment restrictions, a trustee can be given a wide range of investment options, increasing the income potential of the trust.

To help secure your child's financial future, particularly if you have limited assets, you can grant the trustee the ability to spend the principal of the trust in emergency situations. During normal situations the trustee spends only the income generated from the trust property in order to preserve the longevity of the trust.

If you rely on government benefits for the support and maintenance of your child, and therefore the net worth and income of the disabled person are limited for eligibility purposes, the trustee's control should be exclusive. *The mentally disabled beneficiary should not have the power to demand principal or income distributions from the trust property.* In this way, the beneficiary will not be considered to have any *legal estate* in the trust property and the state will not be able to seize the assets to pay for services rendered or use them in determining eligibility. It is critical that the beneficiary's interest in the trust does not fall within the definition of an "estate," because many state statutes mandate reimbursement from the disabled person's estate. Even for families not relying on government aid, the disabled should not be able to demand principal.

• A "spendthrift clause," also known as a "protection from claims by strangers" clause, should be included in every trust established for the benefit of a mentally disabled beneficiary. A spendthrift clause in a trust agreement provides that the beneficiary cannot voluntarily dispose of the principal or the income of the trust before it is paid to the beneficiary. As a result, the trust principal and income are protected from creditors of the beneficiary. Without a spendthrift provision in the trust, a beneficiary, without actually having the money, could buy a new Mercedes Benz and hold the trust responsible.

When a spendthrift clause is used in a trust, a clear statement of the purpose of the trust is again important. The purpose statement should call attention to the need to protect the beneficiary who is mentally disabled and might unwisely incur debts and liabilities. The purpose statement should make clear that the creator of the trust intended to limit the ownership of the beneficiary.

Unfortunately, a spendthrift provision does not necessarily render a trust immune to claims of creditors. State laws vary as to whether public or private creditors can seize trust assets when a spendthrift clause is used to protect a mentally disabled beneficiary. Generally, spendthrift provisions provide better protection against private creditors than public or governmental creditors. Although it might not work, it should be included anyway. Depending on your state's laws, your lawyer will know how strongly the spendthrift provision should be relied on.

• You can include a trust provision which automatically terminates the trust and distributes the trust property to the remaindermen (the future beneficiaries) in the event the government attempts to seize the assets of the trust property for reimbursement for services rendered to the disabled person. There is not sufficient law to determine whether this provision would be enforceable.

In any event, it is important to include a provision in the trust that states a concern for the remaindermen of the trust. In this way, one can argue if challenged in court that it would be unfair to the remaindermen for the state to seize the trust property for services rendered to the disabled beneficiary.

• You should select a trustee very carefully. The trustee must be a person or an organization that is able to effectively manage the trust property in order to provide for the needs of the disabled beneficiary. The quality of your child's life may depend in large part on the skill, experience, and integrity of the trustee. Selecting a proper trustee will be discussed in detail in a later section.

• Do not assume the trustee understands the unique needs and abilities of your disabled child. Inform the trustee personally of your preferences for care and write these preferences in the trust document—being careful not to be too restrictive.

HOW MUCH MONEY SHOULD BE PUT INTO THE TRUST?

You should consider the following factors in determining what assets you will place in trust for your child:

• Estimate how long your child will live and need care.

• Consider how much money you can afford to tie up in the trust.

• Calculate the amount of government benefits available to your child and attempt to calculate the future trend in available benefits.

• Calculate the yearly cost of care for your disabled child (do not forget to build in an inflation rate).

• Determine what amounts of money you want to give to people other than your disabled child.

• Calculate the interest and capital appreciation generated from the trust property.

SELECTING A TRUSTEE

As a parent, you may choose to act as trustee when you create a trust for your child. It will still be necessary for you to select a trustee to serve in the event of your death. In choosing a competent trustee you should select a person who

• Understands the unique needs and abilities of your mentally handicapped child.

• Will carry out your wishes after your death.

• Can manage and invest trust property skillfully.

- Will be likely to live as long as your child.

- Has no conflict of interests with your disabled child.

THE CORPORATE TRUSTEE

A corporate trustee is usually a financial institution such as a bank or a savings and loan association. There are three major advantages offered by a corporate trustee:

1. Corporate trustees can be relied on to manage and invest skillfully the trust property. Usually, banks acting as trustees have seven or eight different investment plans. You should inquire about these because each plan is designed for a different financial objective and each plan invests differently in terms of risk, income generation, and capital appreciation.

2. Corporate trustees are independent and impartial and will attempt to treat all the trust beneficiaries fairly.

3. Corporate trustees do not die. They will provide a continuity of financial management for the entire lifetime of your disabled child.

However, the corporate trustee also has some disadvantages. A major disadvantage is that most bank trustees require a minimum trust size of $50,000 to $200,000. A second disadvantage is that banks charge an annual fee for their trust services and often an additional charge when the trust terminates. Finally, though the bank's impartiality was cited as an advantage, it may also be a disadvantage if the bank, as trustee, is not interested in being a friend and advocate for your disabled child (particularly after your death).

THE INDIVIDUAL TRUSTEE

An individual trustee is, as you would expect, an individual who manages the money in a trust. Anyone who cares about the disabled person and can manage the trust property can be an individual trustee. The individual trustee can be someone with a strong, personal concern for the disabled person; often this trustee is a relative or close friend. There is no minimum trust size because an individual trustee will manage the trust property regardless of its size. And, an individual trustee, especially if a relative, may not charge for services.

However, there is another side of the coin. The individual trustee may not be able to manage money as skillfully as a bank. And, unlike a bank, the individual trustee may die before the disabled beneficiary. To safeguard against this problem, you should appoint several trustees who will manage the trust one after the other if one dies. The last trustee can be given the power to appoint his or her successor. In this way, there will always be a trustee of your choice to care for your disabled child.

Another disadvantage of an individual trustee is the potential for a conflict of interest. Avoid selecting another beneficiary under the trust, such as a brother or sister of the disabled person, to be the individual trustee. Such a selection would place the brother or sister in a conflict of interest between distributing assets to the disabled person or to himself or herself. Similarly, avoid selecting an individual trustee who will receive the trust property after the death of your disabled child. This again would place the trustee in a conflict of interest between investing the trust property in income-producing assets for the beneficiary, or investing in assets that will have long-term capital appreciation and will favor the eventual recipient of the trust, or in this case the trustee. A good trust will not place too great a reliance on the selflessness of human nature.

As a safeguard, you can require the trustee to make an "accounting" to an independent third party. The accounting provides information on investments, taxes, distributions, and the personal well-being of the disabled person.

CO-TRUSTEES

Co-trustees can often solve the problems associated with both the corporate and individual trustee. In fact, it is possible to combine the strengths of both kinds of trustee by naming a bank and an individual as co-trustees. You select the bank trustee to manage and invest the trust property and name an individual trustee to pay for services and goods for the disabled person. The bank trustee manages money expertly and the individual trustee understands the needs of the disabled beneficiary. The individual trustee can also act as the personal advocate for the disabled person.

Appointing co-trustees can also guard against conflict of interest. If your possible trustee candidates are relatives of your disabled child who stand in financial conflict of interest, appoint two of them as co-trustees with equal power. For example, you have two sons and a disabled daughter. In the trust document the sons will receive the trust property after the death of your daughter. Both sons love their sister but you are worried that one of them might be tempted to skimp on goods and services for the sister in order to inherit more money after her death. As a safeguard, you can appoint one son and the surviving parent as co-trustees. Or appoint one son and an independent third person as co-trustees. In this way, you can guard against potential conflict of interests but still have a loving, concerned relative as trustee for your disabled daughter. However, this arrangement of co-trustees with equal power does carry the possibility of a stalement when both trustees are in disagreement as to which course of action to take.

DUTIES OF A TRUSTEE

Remember that as the creator of the trust you can spell out the duties and powers of the trustee. Do not throw away this advantage by using a standardized trust form. Have your attorney draft a trust that gives the trustee detailed instructions for the care of your disabled child. The future trustee will appreciate this guidance.

The trustee can be responsible for both the financial and personal concerns of your handicapped child. The financial duties of the trustee fall into two categories. The first type of duty deals with the administration of the trust, such as investing the trust property, paying taxes on the income, and keeping accurate records of all payments, expenses, and investments. You can grant the trustee broad discretion in investment decisions or restrict the trustee's alternatives to certain types of investments. Given the constantly fluctuating economy, it is better to select a trustee you are confident in and to give the trustee broad investment powers than it is to restrict the trustee's investment powers. Even if you grant the trustee broad investment powers, the law requires the trustee to act as a *conservor* of assets and to invest the trust property prudently.

The second type of financial duty includes paying out principal or income for the beneficiary. In carrying out these distributive duties, the trustee complies with your explicit directions, and makes those decisions which are left to the trustee's own judgment.

One of the trustee's responsibilities that you can control is what the trustee can spend money on. As discussed earlier, if you are trying to protect the trust property from potential governmental creditors and to maintain your child's eligibility for governmental benefits, you will direct the trustee to have total control over the distribution of principal and income. You will permit the trustee to spend money on goods and services that supplement but never duplicate governmental benefits. You will not permit your disabled child to demand either principal or income from the trust.

In the trust document, you can direct the trustee not only to manage the financial affairs of your child, but also to take interest in the personal needs of your child. You can direct the trustee to visit your child regularly and assess the services your child needs. You might have one trustee manage the trust property and have another trustee buy goods and services for your child. If the trustee obtains governmental financial assistance, the money *cannot be commingled* with the trust property.

You can control many elements to protect your child after your death. However, you cannot control the future. You cannot predict the growth of your child, the future needs of your child, the future costs of care for your child. Therefore, you must grant the trustee enough flexibility to care for your child in a changing world.

OTHER TRUSTS

Trusts come in many types and variations. You can combine any of these types into your own individually tailored trust with the help of your lawyer. You must consider many objectives and factors before you establish a trust. You should consider

• Whether you want control over the trust property while you are alive.

• Whether you are concerned about protecting the trust property from governmental creditors.

• Whether you are concerned about maintaining your son or daughter's eligibility for governmental aid.

• Whether you are concerned about taxes and need a tax shelter.

• How many beneficiaries there are and in what proportion you wish to distribute the trust property to them.

• Whether you need one trust for several beneficiaries or a

separate trust for each beneficiary. Multiple trusts cost more to draft.

• Whether you want the trust to begin working while you are living or after your death.

Your job in the estate planning process is to understand your objectives and convey this information to your lawyer. Do not expect your attorney to guess your objectives for caring for your child. Explain your intentions to your lawyer in simple, everyday language. Your lawyer's job will be to convert your objectives into the right legal package.

Described below in general terms are various types of trusts and their characteristics. Remember that many of these trust characteristics can be combined in a single trust that is designed for your particular estate plan.

Living trust. A living trust is created and goes into effect during your lifetime. Living trusts are often created with relatively small sums; frequently the bulk of the trust property transfers into the trust at your death by means of a pour-over provision in your will.

By nominally funding the trust when you create it, you keep control of assets that may otherwise have been tied up in the trust. At your death, the assets you designate are transferred into the trust for the benefit of your disabled child. In addition, the assets that transfer into the trust are not subject to the probate proceedings. At the time of your death assets transfer automatically into the trust for the benefit of your child without probate delay or probate costs.

Testamentary trust. Trusts established by the creator in his or her will to go into effect after his death are called testamentary trusts. Testamentary trusts are less common today. However, they can be appropriate in certain circumstances. For example, a young couple with a handicapped child cannot afford to set up a living trust. However, they do have significant life insurance policies. This couple might state in their wills that if they both die in a common accident, all their assets, including the life insurance proceeds, will be placed in trust for the benefit of their handicapped child.

Revocable trust. In a revocable trust the creator retains the right to alter, amend, or terminate the trust. At any time prior to the death of the creator of the revocable trust, the creator can add or withdraw trust property, change the trustee, or even name additional beneficiaries.

The revocable trust gives the parents great flexibility in changing the terms of the trust depending upon the changing needs of their disabled child. For example, if the spendthrift laws in your state change, you can adjust the terms of the trust to meet that circumstance. The revocable trust also allows parents to monitor a trustee while the parents are living. If you are unhappy with the trustee, you can appoint a new one before your death. The revocable trust permits parents to increase or decrease the size of the trust property as the financial needs of the beneficiary change. It also allows the parents to invade the trust principal or receive trust income. The trust property, however, remains a part of the creator's taxable assets. A provision for amendment should be specifically stated in whatever type of revocable trust is created.

Irrevocable trust. With an irrevocable trust the creator cannot terminate or alter the trust provisions. The irrevocable trust offers some tax advantages. The trust property is not generally calculated as part of the creator's taxable estate if the creator does not have the right to control the trust or receive any of the trust property or income. The income of the trust will be taxed according to the disabled beneficiary's tax bracket rather than that of the creator of the trust. You should discuss the tax implications with your attorney, however, because a gift tax might be applied to an irrevocable trust. You would have to weigh the amount of gift tax against the income tax savings to decide if an irrevocable trust is cost-effective for you.

Simple trust. In a simple trust the trust agreement requires that all of the income must be distributed to the beneficiary.

Complex trust. In a complex trust the trustee is granted discretion as to when and how much of the income and principal are to be distributed to the beneficiary.

Discretionary trust. If a trust agreement allows the trustee to use his or her judgment (discretion) in distributing or withholding the trust income and/or principal to the beneficiary, it is sometimes referred to as a discretionary trust.

Sprinkling trusts. The sprinkling trust allows the trustee to have the decision-making power to distribute income and principal among a number of beneficiaries. The trustee controls the timing and the amount of the distributions. The trustee can distribute larger amounts of income and principal to the beneficiary who is in the most need. For example, you might create a sprinkling trust for your five children, one of whom is handicapped. In one year, your handicapped child might need an operation and the trustee would distribute a larger portion of the trust income to pay for the operation. In another year, the trustee might spend the larger portion of the income on another child for college tuition. In a third year, the trustee might distribute the income equally among the five children.

This sprinkling trust can be combined with "supplemental benefits" language. The trustee has discretion to distribute principal and income according to the needs of the healthy beneficiaries and is restricted to distribute funds to the mentally disabled beneficiary only in excess of funds supplied by government agencies. It is believed that this type of trust would be very difficult for the state to collect from because not only does it contain the "supplemental benefits" language but it would also be unfair to the other beneficiaries for the state to seize the trust assets. This type of language could be drafted something like this:

This trust shall be designated "The Smith Children's Trust," and the beneficiaries shall be George Smith, Sally Smith, and Timothy Smith. Upon the death of my wife, or upon my death if she predeceases me, the trustee shall hold the balance of my estate for the benefit of the beneficiaries above-named in a common fund and, as to George Smith and Sally Smith, shall pay as later defined whatever part of the income and/or principal the trustee deems necessary and desirable for the comfortable care, support, maintenance, medical care, welfare, and education of the beneficiaries. As to my son, Timothy Smith, the trustee may make payment only for extra and supplemental care, maintenance, support, and education in addition to and over and above the benefits Timothy Smith otherwise receives as a result of his handicap or disability from any local, state, or federal government or from any private agency, any of which provides services or benefits to handicapped persons. It is the express purpose of the grantor to use the trust estate only to supplement other benefits received by this beneficiary.

Short-term trust. The short-term trust, also called the Clifford or reversionary trust, can accumulate money for a disabled person and provide a tax shelter for the creator of the trust. The creator of the trust places assets into a trust as a temporary gift to the disabled beneficiary. Until the creator of the trust gets the trust property back, the income generated from the trust property is taxable to the beneficiary, who is presumably in a lower tax bracket. The net effect is that for the term of the trust the creator pays no tax on the trust assets while generating income for the disabled person that is taxed at a lower rate.

Many restrictions are placed on short-term trusts. The term of the trust must be more than ten years or for the life of the creator, which is why the trust is nicknamed the "ten years and a day" trust. During these ten years, the creator of the trust cannot retain any significant powers of ownership. Only certain types of assets can be the trust property. Since many regulations must be complied with for this trust to be a legal tax shelter, consult your attorney who can draft a proper one for you.

Insurance trust. An insurance trust designates a trust fund as beneficiary of one or more life insurance policies. The proceeds of the policies fund the trust at the creator's death. If certain conditions are met, the proceeds of the insurance policies pass directly to the trust and the trust beneficiaries without being included in the creator's estate.

Grantor trust. A grantor trust is a trust in which the grantor (creator) retains such a degree of control over the principal or income of the trust that he is considered to be the owner of the trust and the income. Generally, for example, a grantor trust is revocable; thus the grantor is taxed on the trust income even if it is distributed to someone else.

Marital or estate trust. Under a marital or estate trust, the property passes to the trustee for the benefit of the spouse. The spouse receives the income regularly from the property and may draw upon or exercise a "power of appointment" over the principal.

A power of appointment is the right given to a beneficiary to designate who will receive the benefit of the trust property next. The benefit of the property can be awarded either presently or after the original beneficiary has died. A "limited" power of appointment restricts the designation to certain people or classes of people. A "general" power of appointment includes no such restrictions.

A marital trust which meets the above requirements will generally qualify for the marital tax deduction.

Charitable remainder trust. A charitable remainder trust usually distributes the income generated by the trust principal to a designated beneficiary, with the principal to pass to a qualified non-profit organization when the beneficiary dies. A *charitable remainder unitrust* distributes a percentage of income each year based on the value of assets in the trust. A *charitable remainder annuity trust* distributes a set percentage of income each year.

Joint interest trust. In a joint interest trust, jointly held property is placed in a revocable or irrevocable trust by the owners. The trustee issues shares representing each owner's proportionate ownership. The trustee distributes income from the trust property to beneficiaries as directed in the trust agreement. When one creator dies, his or her share of the trust property passes to his or her beneficiary as the trust agreement dictates. The beneficiary can be either the other creator or someone else.

Residual trust (sometimes called a non-marital or family trust). In a residual trust, estate property that has not otherwise been distributed (the residue of the trust) passes to the trustee with special instructions as to income and principal. Often, the income from the residual trust will be designated for the benefit of the surviving spouse, with the principal amount to be passed on to the children when the surviving spouse dies. Property in such a trust is taxed as part of the creator's estate, but is not generally taxed again at the death of the beneficiary.

LAW REVIEW ARTICLES AND CASE LAW

The following articles and law cases will further assist your lawyer in establishing a trust designed to protect the future of your mentally disabled child.

Articles.
Annot: *Incompetent—Trust—Claim for Support,* 92 ALR 2d 838 (1963).
Crown, *Planning for Emotionally Disabled Beneficiaries,* 119 T & E 38, (1980).
Frolik, *Estate Planning for Parents of Mentally Disabled Children,* 40 U. Pitt. L. R. 305 (1979*).*

Masey, *Protecting the Mentally Incompetent Child's Trust Interest From State Reimbursement Claims,* 58 Denver L.J. 557 (1981).
Note, *Avoiding An Unwanted Invasion of Trust,* 45 Albany L. Rev. 237 (1980).
Restatement of Trusts, 1, sec. 157.
Restatement of Trusts, 1, 187(j) (1935).
Rotman, *Estate Planning for Families of the Handicapped.*
Scott on Trusts, 2d Ed., Vol. II, sec. 157.2, pp. 1115-1119.
Speisman, *Payment Responsibility for Medical Services Rendered in Illinois Public Mental Health Institutions,* Ill. B.J., Mr., '82, 450-3.

Case Law.

Barnhart v. Barnhart, 415 Ill. 303 (1953).
Bee v. Edinburn, 44 Ill. App. 3d 13, 357 N.E. 2d 845 (1976).
Bridgeport—City Trust Co. v. Beach, 174 A. 308 (1934).
Bridgeport v. Reilly, 47 A. 2d 865 (1946).
Bureau of Support v. Kreitzer, 16 Ohio St. 2d 147, 243 N.E. 2d 83 (1968).
City of Bridgeport v. Reilly, 133 Conn. 31, 47 A. 2d 865 (1946).
Commonwealth v. Montgomery Trust Co., 50 Pa. 282, 59 Montg. Co. LR 213 (1943).
Constanza v. Verona, 48 N.J. Super. 355, 137 A. 2d 614 (1958).
Continental National Bank v. Sever, 393 Ill. 81, 65 N.E. 2d 385 (1946).
Department of Mental Health v. Coty, 38 Ill. 2d 597, 232 N.E. 2d 681 (1967)
Department of Mental Health v. Pauling, 47 Ill. 2d 269, 265 N.E. 2d 159 (1970).
Department of Public Welfare v. Foster, 13 Ill. 2d 55, 147 N.E. 2d 319 (1958).
Department of Public Welfare v. Haas, 15 Ill. 2d 204, 154 N.E. 2d 265 (1958).
Department of Public Welfare v. Meek, 264 Ky. 771, 95 S.W. 2d 599 (1936)
England v. England, 223 Ill. App. 549 (1922).
Estate v. Escher, 407 N.Y.S. 2d 106 (Surr. Ct. 1978).
First National Bank of Maryland v. Department of Health, 399 A. 2d 891 (Md. Ct. App. 1979).
Grabois v. Grosner, 363 F. 2d 979 (D.C. Cir. 1966).
Grames v. Norris, 3 Ill. 2d 107 (1954).
Hanford v. Glancy, 183 A. 271 (N.H. 1936).

In re Cooke's Estate, 47 N.Y.S. 2d 844 (Surr. Ct. 1944).

In re Emmon's Will, 59 N.Y.S. 2d 264 (Surr. Ct. 1946).

In re Estate of Ross, 96 Misc. 2d 463, 409 N.Y.S. 2d 201 (Surr. Ct. 1978).

In re Gruber's Will, 122 N.Y.S. 2d 654 (1953).

In re Hinkley's Estate, 15 Cal. Rptr. 570 (1961).

In re Hohenshielt's Estate, 105 Pa. Super. 18, 159 A. 71 (1932).

In re Johnson's Estate, 17 Cal. Rptr. 909 (Ct. App. 1962).

In re Spangler, 3 Pa. D&C 616, 36 York Leg. Rec. 157 (1923).

In re Walter's Case, 278 Pa. 421, 123 A. 408.

Johnson v. Sarver, 350 Ill. App. 565, 113 N.E. 2d 578 (1953).

Keller v. Keller, 284 Ill. App. 198, 1 N.E. 2d 773 (1936).

Kough v. Hoehler, 413 Ill. 409, 109 N.E. 2d 177 (1952).

Lackman v. Department of Mental Hygiene, 156 Cal. App. 2d 674 (Dist. Ct. 1958).

Martin v. McClure, 318 Ill. 585. 149 N.E. 489 (1925).

Nichols v. Eaton, 23 L.E. 254 (1875).

Reilly v. State, 177 A. 528 (Ct. 1935).

State v. Boyer, No. 81-169, (1st Dist. Feb. 11). *cert. denied,* (1982).

State v. Commercial National Bank of Peoria, No. 76E 551, 79L 4372 (1980).

State v. Rubion, 158 Tex. 43, 308 S.W. 2d 4 (1957).

State v. Truitt, 78 CH 1806 (1979).

United States v. Dallas National Bank, 152 F. 2d 582 (5th Cir. 1946).

United States Trust Co. of New York v. Jones, 414 Ill. 265, Ill N.E. 2d 144 (1953).

Wallace v. Foxwell, 250 Ill. 616, 95 N.E. 985 (1911).

Will of Wright, 12 Wis. 2d 375, 107 NW 2d 146 (1961).

Wingard v. Harrison, 337 Ill. 387, 169 N.E. 232 (1929).

Chapter 4
Government Benefits

This chapter deals with various benefits to which your disabled child may be entitled from the federal government. These benefits are not charity, but claims to government entitlements. Many of these programs and services are federally funded and administered by the state governments. Only the government programs to which the disabled person is entitled as a result of his or her disability will be discussed. This chapter will not cover government benefits such as senior citizen's benefits that a disabled person may be entitled to regardless of his or her disability. Nor will it discuss the infinite array of private, non-governmental services, facilities, and programs that provide tremendous support to disabled persons. Although these programs are not discussed here, parents should constantly hunt for programs, services, and facilities for their disabled child, regardless of the funding sources.

The governmental benefits discussed in this chapter are based on different underlying principles. Generally, these programs may be classified into three types—public assistance, social insurance, and in-kind benefits. Public assistance programs, such as Supplemental Security Income (SSI) for disabled persons, are funded by general tax revenues and assist persons whose resources and income levels are inadequate to maintain a minimum standard of living. Social insurance programs, like Social Security, are funded by the insured who is entitled to benefits. Benefits "in-kind" are services (such as vocational rehabilitation), goods, or facilities which have a cash-value, but are available free or at a reduced cost to the disabled person.

Throughout this book the relationship between governmental benefits and private income is emphasized. Families who rely on government benefits must be careful not to violate the eligibility requirements for the various programs. Most government benefit programs have eligibility criteria. For the eligibility purposes of most federal public assistance programs, only the income and resources of the *adult* disabled person are taken into account, not the family's resources or income. Therefore, when the disabled person is over 18 years of age, families that need government benefits must avoid giving directly to the disabled person any assets which may disqualify him or her for benefits. On the other hand, if the family does not need to rely on government benefits for cash payments, long-term public residential care, and social needs, the family may not need to worry about eligibility for government programs. However, the vast majority of families cannot afford the cost of private care for their disabled child.

The first section of the chapter will demonstrate how families of the disabled and their advisors must learn to provide for the disabled person in ways that will not disqualify that person for public assistance. By using Supplementary Security Income (SSI) as an example, the section will illustrate how to navigate through the maze of eligibility requirements.

The second section is organized around the many areas in which the disabled person needs assistance. This section will briefly discuss various national programs—disability and Social Security, medical benefits, social service programs, education, vocational rehabilitation, employment assistance, civil rights/legal assistance, housing, and transportation. Since many mentally disabled persons are multi-handicapped, many of the government programs discussed provide services for the mentally and physically handicapped. However, this section cannot describe all the government programs nor all the details of each. Moreover, all benefit programs —particularly government programs—change constantly. Before applying, obtain detailed and up-to-date information about benefits and eligibility requirements.

While parents are applying for governmental benefits, they should begin to assemble records and information on the disabled person and file the information for future use. This information will be available to anyone (a surviving parent, a relative, a trustee, a guardian, a case worker) who must help the disabled person apply for public or private benefits in the future. The following information should be on file:

- The disabled person's social security card or number.

- The parents' social security numbers.

- The disabled person's birth certificate.

- Medical records or other clinical information about the disabled person. If reports are not available, list the names and addresses of doctors, hospitals, and clinics that have provided care, and the names and addresses of social workers and administrators of residential facilities who have provided assistance.

- Guardianship orders.

- A copy of any will in which the disabled person is mentioned, including mention in a testamentary guardianship clause.

- Bank books, insurance policies, and other papers that show the disabled person's resources.

- Pay slips, tax returns, and other papers that show the disabled person's income.

- Papers showing admission into a residential facility at any time.

- Income tax W-2 statements of the parents to show coverage under Social Security.

- Information about the parents' income and resources if the disabled person is a minor.

- Information about a spouse's income and resources if the disabled person lives with a spouse.

- If the disabled person is a step-child, a marriage certificate of the parents.

- Veteran's C number or discharge papers of the parent.

- The latest tax bill or assessment notice on any real estate the disabled person owns other than his or her home.

- Motor vehicle registration if the disabled person owns a car.

- Information about the disabled person's eligibility for Supplementary Security Income (SSI).

MAXIMIZING PRIVATE AND PUBLIC ASSISTANCE

A public assistance program, called a "need" program, requires the recipient to show that his or her resources and income are inadequate to meet personal needs. Common examples of public assistance programs are Supplementary Security Income (SSI), which gives cash benefits to the aged, blind, and disabled; Medicaid, which pays for medical benefits; and the Food Stamp Program, which pays for food.

A family's goal should be to give the disabled person money and assets to pay for services for the well-being of the disabled person and at the same time to have the disabled person remain eligible for public assistance benefits such as SSI. At times this requires some manipulation of assets. Is this cheating the government? It is no more cheating than is taking legitimate tax deductions. However, the "legitimacy" of these strategies is not really the issue. The issue, for families with mentally disabled children, is that without this manipulation they are often forced to disinherit their child so that he or she can receive needed public assistance. This necessity only serves to intensify the tragedy of the disability. The other alternative parents have is to provide personally what assistance they can to their disabled child, which frequently results in a reduction or termination of government benefits. Usually neither alternative is sufficient by itself.

This section will demonstrate several strategies families and their advisors should consider when they design a plan to give the disabled person private assistance from the family, while maintaining eligibility for public assistance. These general strategies apply to many public assistance programs even though the specifics of each program vary. For purposes of illustration, SSI will be discussed because it is a major program providing cash payments to the disabled, and because it has less state-to-state variation in requirements than other public assistance programs. Furthermore, SSI eligibility often qualifies the disabled person for other programs. These strategies will make you conscious of the need for analyzing eligibility requirements carefully.

General strategies. The starting point with all public assistance programs is to minimize the disabled person's resources and income as defined by the programs in order to qualify for or increase the disabled person's benefits under these programs.

There are two common strategies for minimizing the disabled person's resources and income:

1. Place resources and income into exempt categories.
2. Place resources into a specially drafted trust.

Exempt resources. "Resources," as defined by SSI, include real estate, personal property, household goods, savings and checking accounts, and stocks and bonds. To be eligible, an individual may have resources (assets) worth up to $1,500, and a couple may have resources worth up to $2,250. If an unmarried child living at home is under 18, part of the parents' assets are considered to be the child's.

Not all resources are counted when SSI determines the amount of a person's resources. Such exempt resources include

● A home and adjacent land, regardless of value, if it is the person's principal place of residence.

● The person's household goods or personal effects that have a total equity value of $2,000 or less. The equity value is the amount of money an item can be sold for. If the total equity of the goods is over $2,000, the excess value is counted.

● The person's car, if it is used by the household for transportation to a job or to a place of regular treatment for a specific medical problem or if it has been modified for use by a handicapped person. If the car is not used for these reasons, the amount of the car's current market value that is above $4,500 will be counted as a resource. The full value of any additional cars owned by the person will be counted unless they are used for self-support.

● Life insurance policies with total face value of $1500 or less to which the person is beneficiary.

● Assets needed by blind or disabled people in order to fulfill a plan for self-support.

If a person gives away or sells any resource for less than its fair market value for the purpose of establishing eligibility for SSI, the uncompensated value will be counted as a resource for 24 months from the date of disposal.

Thus, according to SSI regulations, a disabled person could inherit a home and an automobile and still be eligible for SSI public assistance. The disabled person could also be the beneficiary of a small life insurance policy or a burial policy that is not considered a resource because it does not have a cash value. Only a mildly handicapped person (with the support of someone else) would be capable of maintaining a home or driving a car. But for those people it can be of considerable benefit to have those assets provided without any loss of SSI assistance.

Exempt income. "Income," as the SSI program defines it, includes cash, checks, items received "in-kind" such as food and shelter, and many items which would not be considered income for Federal or other tax purposes. Wages, net earnings from self-employment, earned income tax credits, and/or income received from sheltered workshops are considered earned income. Social Security benefits, workers' or veteran's compensation, annuities, and interest are examples of unearned income. Currently, an individual is eligible for SSI if he or she has income of less than $284.30 a month; a couple is eligible with income of less than $426.40 a month.

If an unmarried child living at home is under 18, some of the parents' income is considered to be the child's. Allowances are made for the parents' work and living expenses and for other children living at home. After these allowances are deducted from the parents' income, the remaining amount is counted as the child's income. For children over 18 years, SSI counts only the child's income, even if he or she is still a dependent.

Because income includes so many different types of funds from so many different sources, what is counted and what is not counted toward eligibility become very complex. Although the list of rules is long, it is important to be aware of the types of income that are outside the eligibility requirements. Many of the types of income that are *not* counted include:

- $20 a month of earned or unearned income (except unearned income such as Veteran's disability, pensions, or assistance based on need)

- $65 a month of earned income plus one-half of earned income over $65 a month or, if there is no unearned income, $85 a month of earned income plus one-half of the remainder.

- Irregular or infrequent earned income if it totals no more than $10 a month.

- Irregular or infrequent unearned income if it totals no more than $20 a month.

- Earnings (up to $1,200 a quarter, but not more than $1,620 a year) of an unmarried child who is a student under 22.

- Tuition and fees of grants, scholarships, fellowships and government loans for education.

● One-third of child support payments received by an eligible child from an absent parent.

● Income necessary for fulfillment of an approved plan for a blind or disabled person to achieve self-support.

● Impairment-related work expenses for an eligible person who is disabled or blind.

● Assistance based on need from a state or local municipal subdivision.

● Food stamp assistance.

● Housing assistance from Federal housing programs run by state and local subdivisions.

● Benefits, compensation, or items from ACTION programs run by state and local subdivisions.

● Incentive allowances and certain types of reimbursement for individuals in training under CETA programs administered by state and local subdivisions.

Any of these can be used to provide the disabled person with additional funds without jeopardizing benefits.

Resources in trust. A resource is defined as

cash or other liquid assets or any real or personal property that an individual (or spouse if any) owns and could convert to cash to be used for his support and maintenance. If the individual has the right, authority or power to liquidate the property or his share of the property, it is considered a resource. If a property right cannot be liquidated, the property will not be considered a resource of the individual (or spouse).

According to this definition of a resource, if the disabled person's resources are placed into a properly drafted trust, the person can benefit from the trust assets and still remain eligible for assistance. Such a trust would restrict the beneficiary's access to the trust property by preventing the disabled person from demanding principal and/or income distributions from the trust property. The trustee would have the authority to make distributions on behalf of the beneficiary. (See Trust Chapter.)

Other strategies. Numerous strategies are possible when maximizing private and public assistance under SSI. A few of these are

• Because earned income causes a lesser reduction in benefits than unearned income, when possible characterize income as earned rather than unearned. For example, if possible, income from rental property should be classified as earned.

• Pay creditors of the disabled person directly. For purposes of SSI eligibility, income is defined as

the receipt by an individual of any property or service which he can apply either directly or by sale or conversion to meeting his basic needs for food, clothing, and shelter.

Any gift to the disabled person other than food, clothing, or shelter which cannot be converted into cash, does not constitute income for SSI eligibility purposes. Accordingly, parents should pay creditors of the disabled person directly rather than give money to the disabled person to pay for bills other than food, clothing, or shelter. For example, a parent could pay a telephone bill for the handicapped child directly to the phone company. This payment is not considered income to the disabled person. However, if the parent gives the disabled child money to pay the telephone company, that money constitutes income to the child.

• If the disabled person receives income from any source, such as a trust, transfer the bulk of the income in one quarter of the year. Generally, income is counted in the quarter it is received. Therefore, assuming the disabled beneficiary meets the asset limitation for eligibility, the income from the trust would only reduce SSI proceeds for one quarter. Benefits for the other three quarters would not be changed.

• Place unearned income into the classification of infrequent income. According to SSI eligibility rules, $60 a quarter of irregular or infrequent unearned income is excluded from income. Income is considered infrequent if the disabled person receives it less than twice a quarter.

• Have the disabled person *use* a consumer item rather than *own* it. If the disabled person does not own the consumer item it cannot be converted to cash, therefore it is not income for SSI purposes. The use of a consumer item will not be considered income if it does not provide a basic need—food, clothing, or shelter.

This section has suggested some strategies to consider in order to maximize public and private assistance to help secure the future of a disabled person. It should also be clear that any such strategy must be based on a thorough understanding of the eligibility requirements of public benefit programs.

DISABILITY AND SOCIAL SECURITY

Generally, an unmarried disabled adult will receive the same benefits as a minor dependent child under Social Security. A disabled adult may receive the Social Security benefits of an insured parent (covered employment requires the payment of "FICA" taxes) after that parent retires, becomes disabled, or dies. The disabled person need not have worked under Social Security because benefits are paid on the father's or mother's Social Security work record. Adults are considered "disabled and eligible to receive Social Security benefits if they have severe physical or mental impairments which began before the age of 22 and which keep them from doing any substantial gainful work as adults. A disabled adult can receive benefits after the death of the insured parent as high as 75% of the insured parent's primary insurance amount based on average earnings.

If the disabled person is receiving Social Security benefits before the age of 18, an application to continue benefits should be made at least 3 months before the disabled person becomes 18. In this way, the benefit payments will continue without interruption. If the disability begins between the ages of 18 and 22, an application should be filed at the same time an insured parent starts getting retirement or disability benefits, or dies. Social Security places no age limit on filing an application if the disability began before the age of 22.

When processing an application for a disabled adult, the Social Security office will ask for medical evidence that the disability is severe, that it began before the age of 22, and that it will continue into the future. For proof of disability, the parent should present a report from a doctor or from a care facility where the disabled person resides. In addition, the parent will have to show the age of the disabled person and the relationship to the insured worker. A birth certificate will show both age and relationship.

When processing the application, the Social Security office will probably contact the state vocational rehabilitation agency. The vocational rehabilitation agency will review the applicant's eligibility for vocational services such as job counseling, job training, and

(Note: If you want more information about the SSI program, contact any Social Security office. The phone number is listed under Social Security Administration.)

placement. If the rehabilitation services are offered and refused, the Social Security office might deny benefits.

It should be noted that in some cases a mentally disabled person can receive benefits as an insured rather than as a dependent. Under new laws, the disabled person can obtain insured status under Social Security laws, even while working in a sheltered workshop, if Social Security taxes are paid.

MEDICAL BENEFITS

Medicare. Medicare is a two-part federal health insurance program administered by the Social Security program. It is designed to pay the cost of health care for people over the age of 65 and for disabled persons who are under the age of 65 and have been entitled to receive Social Security disability benefits for a total of two or more years; or need kidney dialysis treatments or a kidney transplant. Eligibility for Medicare is not based on financial need.

The Medicare program has two parts:

Part A includes hospital insurance benefits that help pay for care in the hospital and for related health care services after leaving the hospital, including skilled nursing or rehabilitation care at facilities that have been certified by Medicare. There are no premiums for the hospital insurance. However, recipients do have to pay a small portion of the hospital bill. (See following chart for details.)

Part B includes medical insurance benefits that help cover the costs of medical services such as physician's services, home health care, and outpatient hospital treatment. To be eligible for Part B a person must be enrolled in Part A and must pay monthly premiums. Under Part B, an insured individual must pay a $75 deductible. Generally, Medicare will cover 80% of the costs, and the insured will pay the remaining 20%. Many individuals purchase supplementary insurance from another source to pay the 20% that Medicare Part B will not cover.

Further information on Medicare is available from your local Social Security Office, or by writing to

Health Care Financing Administration, Inquiries Branch
Rm. 1-N-4, East Lowrise Bldg.
Baltimore, Md. 21235

The following chart will demonstrate which medical services are covered by Medicare and how the benefits are paid:

MEDICARE—HOSPITAL INSURANCE BENEFITS (PART A)

FOR COVERED SERVICES—EACH BENEFIT PERIOD

SERVICE	BENEFIT	MEDICARE PAYS	YOU PAY**
HOSPITALIZATION . . . Semiprivate room and board, general nursing and miscellaneous hospital services and supplies. Includes meals, special care units, drugs, lab tests, diagnostic X-rays, medical supplies, operating and recovery room, anesthesia and rehabilitation services.	First 60 days	All but $260	$260
	61st to 90th day	All but $65 a day	$65 a day
	91st to 150th day*	All but $130 a day	$130 a day
	Beyond 150 days	Nothing	All costs
	A Benefit Period begins on the first day you receive service as an inpatient in a hospital and ends after you have been out of the hospital or skilled nursing facility for 60 days in a row.		
POSTHOSPITAL SKILLED NURSING FACILITY CARE . . . In a facility approved by Medicare. You must have been in a hospital for at least 3 days and enter the facility within 30 days after hospital discharge.	First 20 days	100% of approved amount	Nothing
	Additional 80 days	All but $32.50	$32.50
	Beyond 100 days	Nothing	All costs
	MEDICARE AND PRIVATE INSURANCE WILL NOT PAY FOR MOST NURSING HOME CARE. YOU PAY FOR CUSTODIAL CARE AND MOST CARE IN A NURSING HOME.		
HOME HEALTH CARE	Unlimited as medically necessary	Full cost	Nothing
BLOOD	Blood	All but first 3 pints	For first 3 pints

* 60 Reserve Days may be used only once; days used are not renewable.
** These figures are for 1982 and are subject to change each year.

MEDICARE—MEDICAL INSURANCE BENEFITS (PART B)

FOR COVERED SERVICES—EACH CALENDAR YEAR

SERVICE	BENEFIT	MEDICARE PAYS	YOU PAY
MEDICAL EXPENSE Physician's services, inpatient and outpatient medical services and supplies, physical and speech therapy, ambulance, etc.	Medicare pays for medical services in or out of the hospital. Some insurance policies pay less (or nothing) for hospital outpatient medical services or services in a doctor's office.	80% of approved amount (after $75 deductible)	$75 deductible* plus 20% of balance of approved amount (plus any charge above approved amount)**
HOME HEALTH CARE	Unlimited as medically necessary	Full cost	Nothing
OUTPATIENT HOSPITAL TREATMENT	Unlimited as medically necessary	80% of approved amount (after $75 deductible)	Subject to deductible plus 20% of balance of approved amount
BLOOD	Blood	80% of approved amount (after first 3 pints)	For first 3 pints plus 20% of balance of approved amount

*Once you have had $75 of expense for covered services in a calendar year, the Part B deductible does not apply to any further covered services you receive in that year.

**YOU PAY FOR charges higher than the amount approved by Medicare unless the doctor or supplier agrees to accept Medicare's approved amount as the total charge for services rendered. (See page 7.)

PRIVATE INSURANCE CHECKLIST	
CURRENT INSURANCE (Premium $) WILL PAY	PROPOSED INSURANCE (Premium $) WILL PAY
If you are considering buying insurance, use the chart on the left and this checklist to help you decide. If you are buying from an agent, ask him or her to help you complete this checklist.	

Medicaid. Medicaid provides health care services to persons with low income. Unlike Medicare, it is a public assistance program based on financial need. Therefore, a person who is eligible for Medicare is not necessarily eligible for Medicaid.

Eligibility for Medicaid depends on the income and resources of the disabled person. Although eligibility requirements for Medicaid vary somewhat from state to state, a disabled person may be eligible if he or she receives Supplementary Security Income (SSI), is on welfare, is blind or disabled, or has medical bills that exceed a certain percentage of annual income.

Medicaid pays for some services that Medicare does not cover. For example, Medicaid can pay for the Medicare Part B deductible.

The medical services covered by Medicaid include

• Necessary medical services provided by physicians, dentists, and other medical professionals.

• Hospital care.

• Home health care services, including nursing homes and long-term care in public or private licensed intermediate care facilities (ICF), if the state includes the ICF in its medical plan. The majority of the states cover ICF services for the mentally retarded.

• Out-patient or clinical services.

• Drugs, eyeglasses, home health aids, medical supplies, and prosthetic appliances.

To obtain further information about applying for Medicaid, or to get information about eligibility requirements, contact your local Medicaid office, usually through your state's Department of Public Aid. To obtain an informative book on Medicaid write to

Medical Services Administration
U.S. Department of Health, Education, and Welfare
Washington, D.C.

Maternal and Child Health and Crippled Children's Services. Under Title V of the Social Security Act, the states are granted money by the Federal Government to provide Maternal and Child Health Services and Crippled Children's Services. Both of these programs provide medical services to the developmentally disabled. The goals of both of these programs are to prevent conditions that might cause disabilities and to treat existing disabilities.

For purposes of these and other federal programs, the definition of a developmental disability is any severe, chronic disability which

A. Is attributable to a mental or physical impairment or impairments,
B. Manifests itself prior to age 22,
C. Will likely continue indefinitely,
D. Results in substantial functional limitations in three or more of the seven major life activities: 1. self-care, 2. receptive and expressive language, 3. learning, 4. mobility, 5. self-direction, 6. capacity for independent living, and 7. economic sufficiency, and
E. Reflects the individual's need for a combination and sequence of special services which are either of extended or life-long duration and which are individually planned and coordinated.

Maternal and Child Health Services. Each state develops its own services for Maternal and Child Health Services Program according to federal guidelines. Some special services which may be offered by the state include

● Maternal and infant care projects. These projects provide complete health care during and after pregnancy.

● Children and youth projects. These projects provide dental care for children.

● Intensive newborn infant care projects.

● Family planning projects.

● Special clinics for developmentally disabled children. The staff at these clinics will diagnose the child's medical condition, develop a treatment plan, give follow-up care for the child, and direct the parents to other medical services.

To find out about your state's Maternal and Child Health Services contact your city, county, or state health department.

Crippled Child Services. Crippled Child Services provide medical treatment to developmentally disabled children. Generally, children must be under 21 years of age to qualify for these services. The medical services vary from state to state. However, typical services include

● Transportation to a clinic.

● Testing for health problems.

- Diagnosis and evaluation of these health problems.

- Treatment for these health problems including treatment by a physician, hospital care, use of equipment to develop your child's skills and abilities, and follow-up care after your child leaves the treatment center. (The necessary equipment itself as well as the medicine is also included.)

Once a child is eligible for these services, the cost of the services depend on the particular state and the income level of the family. However, diagnostic services are provided free to all developmentally disabled children.

Although the eligibility requirements for these programs are complicated, it may still pay to apply. To apply for the services, contact the state Crippled Children Agency, your local health department, or a local public health nurse.

Early Periodic Screening, Diagnosis, and Treatment Program (EPSDT). The EPSDT program screens children from poor families to identify whether health care or related services are necessary. In some states EPSDT services can be provided to children in need regardless of the family's income level.

Children receiving state Aid to Families with Dependent Children benefits, and children whose parents or guardians are receiving Medicaid, and/or local or state public assistance benefits may be eligible for EPSDT programs. Specific eligibility requirements vary from state to state.

EPSDT programs also vary from state to state and are administered by either state public assistance agencies (welfare) or health departments. If your family qualifies under this program, your child can receive the following services:

- A physical examination and a complete health history.

- Tests for different types of blood diseases and for lead-based poisoning.

- Tests to discover whether or not your child has problems with teeth, ears, or eyes.

- Medical treatment for hearing impairment, visual deficiency, or dental problems.

- Other medical services depending on the particular state provider.

To obtain further information on how EPSDT can help your child contact your city, county, or state health department or your local social services, welfare, or Medicaid office.

SOCIAL SERVICE PROGRAMS

Developmental disabilities services. The Developmental Disabilities Assistance and Bill of Rights Act provides financial support to states to help developmentally disabled individuals. The intent of the Act is to "assure that persons with developmental disabilities receive the care, treatment and other services necessary to enable them to achieve their maximum potential . . ." and that these services be provided in the setting least restrictive to personal liberty. At this time it is unclear how enforceable this statement is.

Federal funds are granted to states to provide for the developmentally disabled. The states who seek these funds must meet federal standards with regard to treatment, services, and rehabilitation programming for the developmentally disabled. One of these federal standards requires that the state establish an individual habilitation plan for each developmentally disabled person receiving services.

For eligibility purposes, a developmental disability is defined as any severe, chronic disability which

A. Is attributable to a mental or physical impairment or impairments,

B. Manifests itself prior to age 22,

C. Will likely continue indefinitely,

D. Results in substantial functional limitations in three or more of the seven major life activities: 1. self-care, 2. receptive and expressive language, 3. learning, 4. mobility, 5. self-direction, 6. capacity for independent living, and 7. economic sufficiency, and

E. Reflects the individual's need for a combination and sequence of special services which are either of extended or life-long duration and which are individually planned and coordinated.

To obtain more information about the developmental disabilities services in your state, contact the State Department of Mental Health and Developmental Disabilities.

Title XX. Under Title XX service programs, the states are granted money from the Federal Government to provide social services to disadvantaged and disabled residents. Each state reimbursed under Title XX for providing services must furnish services which meet broad federally-legislated goals. But, within these guidelines, each state decides which services it will give and who will get these services. Although the services vary from state to state, many states provide such services for the handicapped as

- Group living.

- Attendant Care.

- Sheltered Employment.

- Day care for children and adults.

- Home health care.

- Employment and training.

- Recreational services.

- Health and mental health services.

- Legal services.

- Referral services.

The Federal Government has established three categories of eligibility for these Title XX services:

1. Persons eligible on the basis of income maintenance status. These people already qualify to receive Aid to Families with Dependent Children (AFDC), Supplementary Security Income (SSI), or state supplementary payments.

2. Persons eligible on the basis of income status. Not including those eligible on the basis of income maintenance status as described above, these are people whose family's gross monthly income is less than 115% of the median income of a family of four in the state, adjusted for family size.

3. Persons eligible without regard to income. The state can provide information and referral services, family planning services, services to prevent or remedy neglect, abuse, or exploitation of people, without regard to income.

To find out if you can receive Title XX Social Services, you should talk to the agency in your state that administers the Title XX programs. Generally, the state agency that administers these services is either the Department of Welfare, the Department of Social Services, or the Department of Human Services.

EDUCATION

Special education. According to the provisions in the Education for All Handicapped Act, all state and local school districts must provide an appropriate elementary and secondary education for your disabled child from ages 6 through 21. Moreover, states that mandate public education for children age 3 to 5 are required to educate disabled of this age in the least restrictive environment— and, when possible, with the other non-handicapped children. For these public educational services for disabled children, parents do not have to pay any more than parents of non-handicapped children. Furthermore, if the state or local education system places a handicapped child in a private school to meet its educational responsibilities to all children, parents pay no extra costs. Other services provided by public expense include transportation and special educational aids. To obtain further information on special education programs in your state or community, contact your state, county, or local education office.

Project Head Start. Another educational program for young children is Project Head Start. Although the main purpose of Project Head Start is to provide educational opportunities to low-income families, 10 percent of the participants in Head Start must be disabled children. Head Start also has 14 experimental projects to develop a model for serving disabled children in an integrated environment. For more information, look up Project Head Start in the telephone directory, contact your local school board or the Office for Human Development Services of the Department of Health, Education, and Welfare, in Washington, D.C.

Library services. The National Library Service for the Blind and Physically Handicapped has a network of cooperating regional libraries throughout the United States. These libraries provide on free loan a special collection of books, magazines, directories, and educational aids for the disabled. For blind persons, publications are made available in Braille and in recorded form with audio equipment.

To be eligible for these services, the disabled person must be unable to hold a book, or unable to read standard printed material because of blindness, a learning disability, or a physical handicap. To apply for these services, a doctor's report is usually sufficient to qualify the applicant as disabled. For further information on any of these services or to locate a regional library in your area, contact:

National Library Service for the Blind and Physically Handicapped
Library of Congress
Washington, D.C. 20542

Schools for the Deaf and/or Blind. *Elementary and High Schools:* The
Office of Special Education supports post-secondary education of
deaf persons through six major programs across the country and
eight multi-state centers for deaf-blind children. To obtain further
information contact:

Office of Special Education
Department of Education
Washington, D.C. 20202

In the United States, 62 public residential schools for deaf
children accept children from infancy through 12th grade. These
children receive educational training as well as speech therapy, lip
reading, use of hearing aids, and sign language. For more information, contact your local or State Board of Education for the location
of a school within your state.

Gallaudet College: For higher education, the Federal Government
funds Gallaudet College, which provides a liberal arts education to
deaf persons. In addition, to its undergraduate program, Gallaudet
College has a master's program for teacher preparation, and a
research program.

Gallaudet College also runs a secondary school for the deaf for
students from the District of Columbia, Maryland, Virginia, West
Virginia, Pennsylvania, and Delaware. In addition, the college
administers the Kendal Elementary Demonstration School which
experiments in techniques and materials for deaf children and
provides information to other schools for the deaf. For more
information contact

Gallaudet College
7th and Florida Avenue, N.E.
Washington, D.C. 20002

National Technical Institute for the Deaf: Another school of higher
education is the National Technical Institute for the Deaf (NYID)
in Rochester, New York. NTID was created by public law as a
special technical college for deaf students from all states. Frequently, students at NTID can receive financial assistance for tuition
from their state vocational rehabilitation agencies. For more information, contact

Office of Career Opportunities
National Technical Institute for the Deaf
One Lomb Memorial Drive
Rochester, N.Y. 14623

There are approximately 55 special schools for blind children throughout the country. These schools provide educational training from kindergarten to 12th grade. These schools have regular academic curricula as well as special courses in Braille, skills of daily living, orientation, and mobility. Many of these schools will accept blind children with multiple handicaps. For more information on schools in your area, contact your local school district.

VOCATIONAL REHABILITATION

General. The Federal Government provides extensive financial support to the states for vocational rehabilitation. Vocational rehabilitation programs provided by the states help handicapped persons prepare for and find work by providing a wide range of services, financial assistance, and training. Employment ranges from regular jobs to sheltered workshops and home-making. The definition of "handicapped individual" used to determine eligibility for vocational rehabilitations is

any individual who (a) has a physical or mental disability which for such person constitutes or results in a substantial handicap for employment and (b) can reasonably be expected to benefit in terms of employability from vocational rehabilitation.

Vocational rehabilitation programs cannot exclude individuals because of their age or type of disability. However, it should be noted that the definition emphasizes employment potential. Those disabled persons without employment potential as determined by vocational rehabilitation counselors may not qualify for vocational rehabilitation benefits.

The regulations do not require the handicapped person to be in financial need to qualify for the services. In fact, the regulations prohibit the states from charging any individual for evaluation of rehabilitation potential, counseling, referral services, and placement. Each state determines whether or not to establish a financial-need requirement and fees for the other services offered.

Your disabled child's vocational rehabilitation plan will vary depending on personal skills, the counselor's evaluation and recommendations, and the state in which you reside. However, the following vocational rehabilitation services must be available to qualified handicapped persons "as appropriate:"

• A medical examination to determine the nature of the disability, the disabled person's suitability for employment, and the special medical help needed.

• On-going counseling to determine the type of employment most suitable for the disabled person.

• Medical help to reduce or remove a person's disability to improve job performance. This help includes medical, surgical, psychiatric, and hospital services, as well as providing the artificial limbs, braces, hearing devices, and eyeglasses needed on the job.

• Vocational training at trade schools, rehabilitation centers, or at home. These training services also include training materials such as books and tools.

• Educational opportunities, including payment of tuition and expenses for educational efforts necessary to obtain a job.

• Financial assistance during the rehabilitation period for room and board, transportation to and from the job, and other necessary job maintenance assistance.

• Placement in suitable employment.

• Interpreter services for the deaf.

• Services for the blind including reader services, rehabilitation teaching services, and orientation and mobility services.

• Services to members of the disabled person's family to help promote adjustment or rehabilitation of the disabled individual.

• Any goods and services which can be reasonably expected to increase or maintain the disabled person's employability such as occupational licenses, tools, and supplies.

For information on the specific vocational rehabilitation benefits your child might receive, contact the Department of Vocational Rehabilitation in your state.

For blind/deaf persons. Approximately half the states have special vocational rehabilitation units for the blind; the remaining states have established separate commissions that serve only blind persons. These separate organizations are designed to educate a blind client in learning skills for daily living, in orientation and mobility training, in filling out job application forms, and in other rehabilitation needs unique to blind people. These organizations also pay for reader services for blind college students.

The Office of Deafness and Communicative Disorders (ODCD) specializes in rehabilitative services for the deaf. The ODCD develops rehabilitation programs and services for state vocational rehabilitation agencies. The ODCD also develops telecommunications and sensory aids. For more information, contact

The office of Deafness and Communicative Disorders
Room 3416 Switzer Building
Washington, D.C. 20202
(202) 245-0591 (Voice or TTY)

Other alternatives for blind or deaf people are the rehabilitation programs offered by the Helen Keller National Center for Deaf-Blind Youth and Adults. The Federal Government provides funds that help support these programs. To explore your eligibility for the Center's rehabilitation programs, contact

Helen Keller National Center
111 Middle Neck Road
Sands Point, N.Y. 11050
(516) 944-8900 (Voice or TTY)

EMPLOYMENT ASSISTANCE

Employment Security (ES) Offices, also called State Employment Services, exist to help employers find workers, and workers to find jobs. Each ES is required by law to employ a specialist to find jobs for the disabled. For further information, look up Employment Services in the phone book; it should refer you to the state agency responsible for the ES program in your area.

Federal jobs. All federal jobs are announced to the public and most are filled on a competitive basis. However, a small number of special "A" positions are reserved for handicapped persons who are either mentally retarded or severely physically handicapped and are referred by their vocational rehabilitation counselors.

The Office of Personnel Management administers 67 centers to provide federal job information. All centers have selective placement coordinators who provide assistance to handicapped individuals. Furthermore, some of the tests used to screen federal job applicants can be taken by a blind/visually impaired person in Braille, large type, or in recorded form. If the test is not available in any of these formats, the Job Information Center must provide reader assistance to insure that the same test standards are used for all applicants.

For further information about federal jobs for disabled persons contact your nearest Federal Job Information Center listed under U.S. Government in your telephone directory.

State Job Services. State, county, and local governments have their own civil service systems that provide employment services for the disabled. Most states have a Governor's Committee on Employment of the Handicapped, which works with business to create job opportunities for the handicapped. Similarly, State Job Services will provide reader assistance for blind persons applying for a job.

CETA. Many disabled people will meet the eligibility standards of the Comprehensive Employment and Training Program (CETA) which provides jobs for unemployed, underemployed, and the economically disadvantaged. For further information, contact your local State Employment Security Service or your Mayor's office.

Small Business Administration. The Small Business Administration (SBA) may provide low-cost loans to handicapped persons going into business for themselves. If there is no listing for a local SBA office in your telephone directory contact

Small Business Administration
Director, Office of Financing
1441 L Street, N.W.
Washington, D.C. 20416

CIVIL RIGHTS/LEGAL ASSISTANCE

All federally funded institutions are prohibited from excluding handicapped persons from programs or facilities on the basis of the handicap. Therefore, the disabled person has legal rights to education, employment, health care, senior citizen activities, welfare, and any other services which receive federal assistance.

If you feel that any institution receiving federal assistance (e.g. school, hospital, welfare) has violated your rights because of your disability or your child's disability, contact the Office for Civil Rights of the Department of Education (ED) about schools, and the Department of Health and Human Services (HHS) about social services and hospitals in your region.

Region I (Conn., Maine, Mass., N.H., R.I., Vt.)
140 Federal St., 14th Fl.
Boston, MA 02110
ED: (617) 223-6397
HHS: (617) 223-4408

Region II (N.J., N.Y., Puerto Rico, Virgin Islands)
26 Federal Plaza, Rm. 3900
New York, NY 10007
ED: (212) 264-5180
HHS: (212) 264-3313

Region III (Del., D.C., Md., Pa., Va., W. Va.)
3535 Market St., Rm. 6300
Philadelphia, Pa. 19101
ED: (215) 596-6787
HHS: (215) 596-1262

Region LV (Ala., Fla., Ga., Ky., Miss., N.C., S.C., Tenn.)
101 Marietta Street, 27th Floor
Atlanta, Ga. 30323
ED: (404) 221-2954
HHS: (404) 221-2779

Region V (Ill., Ind., Mich., Minn., Ohio, Wis.)
300 South Wacker Drive
Chicago, Ill. 60606
ED: (312) 353-2520
HHS: (312) 886-2300

Region VI (Ark., La., N.M., Okla., Texas)
1200 Main Tower Building, Rm. 1930
Dallas, Tx. 75202
ED: (214) 767-3951
HHS: (214) 767-4056

Region VII (Iowa, Kan., Mo., Neb.)
Twelve Grand Building, 7th Floor
1150 Grand Avenue
Kansas City, Mo. 64106
ED: (816) 374-2223
HHS: (816) 374-2156

Region VIII (Colo., Mont., N.D., S.D., Utah, Wyo.)
1961 Stout Street, Rm. 1194
Denver, Co. 80294
ED: (303) 837-5695
HHS: (303) 837-2024

Region IX (Ariz., Calif., Hawaii, Nev., Guam, Trust Terr.
Pac. Islands, Amer. Samoa)
1275 Market St., 14th Floor
San Francisco, Ca. 94103
ED: (415) 556-8586
HHS: (415) 556-8586

Region X (Alaska, Idaho, Ore., Wash.)
1321 Second Ave.-MS/723
Seattle, Wa. 98101
ED: (206) 442-1922
HHS: (206) 442-0473

HOUSING

Disabled individuals may qualify for a Title I Home Improvement
Loan to remove architectural barriers, hazards, or inconvenient
features in the home. This loan is applied for through a bank which
is insured against loss by the U.S. Department of Housing and
Urban Development (HUD).

Low-income families that support a disabled person might
qualify for rental assistance payments from HUD. These payments
are not considered income for SSI eligibility purposes. For further
information about these housing programs contact

U.S. Department of Housing and Urban Development
Washington, D.C. 20410

TRANSPORTATION

Air. The Federal Aviation Administration (FAA) requires each U.S. airline to submit a national company policy on accessibility and individual services to handicapped individuals. The airline policy must be approved by the FAA. Since these policies vary from airline to airline, a handicapped person should inquire whether or not the airline provides the services needed.

Most airlines will help mentally disabled persons change flights, locate luggage, and find their way through the terminal. When buying the plane ticket at the ticket counter you can request the airlines to enter the fact your child is disabled into their computer. This will insure your child will be taken care of when he or she arrives at the new destination.

You can contact the individual airline and also write for the publication *Access Travel for the Handicapped* which describes design features, facilities, and services at 220 airport terminals worldwide. This booklet is available from

Consumer Information Center
Pueblo, Colorado 81009

Another useful publication, *Access Travel: A Guide to Accessibility of Airport Terminals* is available from

Architectural and Transportation Barriers Compliance Board
Washington, D.C. 20202

Train. Amtrak, a federally subsidized rail system, will become more accessible to handicapped people in the future because every new car will be fitted with special features for the handicapped. To help blind people, the American Foundation for the Blind issues coupons that will give blind travellers and an attendant a 25 percent discount on Amtrak.

You can obtain information about the accessibility of trains and the assistance available to handicapped people by calling Amtrak tollfree. Deaf persons can receive information and make reservations for travel with a teletypewriter by calling (800) 523-6950; in Pennsylvania, call (800) 562-6960.

For further information, request a copy of *Access, Amtrak* for handicapped travellers by writing

Amtrak Public Affairs
400 North Capital St., N.W.
Washington, D.C.

Chapter 5
Taxes

Parents with disabled children should become aware of all the possible tax advantages related to their child's care. These tax benefits will help offset the tremendous costs of caring for a disabled person. This chapter will discuss only the specific medical expense deductions and credits that apply to taxpayers with disabled dependents. The focus will be on the income tax deductions and credits for parents of the disabled and not on the various business tax incentives to promote employment of the disabled. Though the tax laws are tedious, it is important that you take the time to review all of your possible deductions and credits. This chapter tries to simplify the requirements and help you take as large a reduction in your taxes as possible within the law.

A tax deduction is an amount which may be subtracted from your adjusted gross income to arrive at your taxable income. A tax credit is an amount that is subtracted directly from the taxes due. You must figure your medical expense deductions on Schedule A, Form 1040, commonly called the "long form" because you cannot itemize deductions if you use the "short form" 1040A.

Most parents with disabled children deduct larger amounts of medical expenses than ordinary families. As a result, they may draw special notice from the Internal Revenue Service. The IRS computer will single out for review those taxpayers who deduct proportionately higher medical expenses in relation to their income level. To reduce the IRS's suspicions, you can describe your child's disability in a letter written by yourself or your child's doctor and attach it to your tax return. Moreover, you should *record all* medical expenses accompanied by receipts and cancelled checks. Store your receipts and cancelled checks carefully. The key to good tax planning is good record keeping.

To determine your medical deductions ask yourself three questions. First, "whose medical expenses may I deduct?" Second, "which medical expenses are deductible?" Third, "how do I deduct these medical expenses?" After medical expense deductions, this chapter will discuss Child and Disabled Dependent Care Credits.

WHOSE MEDICAL EXPENSES MAY YOU DEDUCT?

The first step is to determine whose medical expenses may be deducted. Individuals may take medical deductions for their spouses and dependents as well as for themselves. It should be noted that you can take an exemption of $1,000 for each dependent. Determining dependents is relatively easy. The following five tests must be met for a person to qualify as your dependent:
1. Support Test.
2. Gross Income Test.
3. Member of Household or Relationship Test.
4. Citizenship Test.
5. Joint Return Test.

Support test. You must provide more than half the dependent's total support during the calendar year. You determine whether you have provided more than half the dependent's support by comparing the amount you contributed to the dependent's support to the entire amount of support received from *all sources,* including the dependent's own funds and government funds.

Total support includes amounts spent to provide food, shelter, clothing, education, medical and dental care, recreation, transportation, and similiar necessities. Some of the sources of support that you may have questions about are explained below.

Medical insurance premiums, including premiums you pay for supplementary Medicare coverage, are included in the total support you provide for the dependent. Medical insurance *benefits* are not part of support. Medicare benefits are not considered support provided by the person who receives the benefits.

Social Security benefit payments. If a dependent receives social security benefits and uses them toward his or her own support, the payments are considered as provided by the dependent.

State benefit payments based on need are considered as support provided by the state and not the parent, unless it is shown otherwise. For example, Aid to Families with Dependent Children

(AFDC) payments are not considered support provided by the parent. They are support provided by the state.

Scholarships received by your dependent, if your dependent is a full-time student, are not included in total support. This includes the value of education, room, and board provided for your dependent. This also applies to scholarships for room, board, and tuition provided for a handicapped child attending a special school. It similiarly would apply to a scholarship for a mentally retarded child to attend an educational institution if the institution certifies that it is making an effort to educate or train the child. For example, your daughter receives a $2,000 scholarship. In the same year you provide $1,800, as her only other support. You may take her as a dependent because the scholarship is not included.

Gross income test. Generally, you may take an exemption or medical deduction for a dependent if that person had less than $1,000 of gross income for the year.

If your child is under 19 years of age at the end of the year, the gross income test does not apply. Your child may have any amount of income and still be your dependent, if the other four tests are met.

If your child is a student, the gross income test does not apply. The child's age does not matter. However, the other four tests must be met. To qualify, your child must be, during some part of each of 5 months of the calendar year (not necessarily consecutive), a full-time student at a school that has a regular teaching staff, course of study, and regularly enrolled student body.

Member of household or relationship test. You may take an exemption or medical deduction for a member of your household who lives with you for the entire year, even if that person is unrelated to you.

Citizenship test. Your dependent must be a U.S. citizen, either resident or national, or a resident of Canada or Mexico for some part of the calendar year in which your tax year begins.

Joint return test. You are not allowed an exemption for your dependent if he or she files a joint return with another person. For example, you supported your daughter for the entire year while her husband was in the armed forces. The couple files a joint return. Even though all the other tests are met, you may not take your daughter as a dependent.

Multiple-Support Agreement. In some situations, more than one person will be supporting the disabled individual. As indicated above, a taxpayer must furnish more than half of the total support of the dependent in this calendar year in order to claim the medical deductions and receive a $1,000 exemption. A Multiple-Support Agreement is used to claim a dependent when two or more people provide more than half a dependent's support, but no one alone provides more than half. In this situation, you may agree that one of you who individually provides more than 10% of the dependent's support may claim medical deductions and the exemption for the dependent. *Only one of the supporters can do this.* Each of the others must file a written statement agreeing not to claim the person as a dependent for these expenses. Form 2120, Multiple Support Declaration, is used for this purpose. This form must be filed with the income tax return of the person who claims the exemption and medical deductions.

Form **2120**	Department of the Treasury—Internal Revenue Service	OMB No. 1545-0071
(Rev. Sept. 1981)	**Multiple Support Declaration**	Expires 8-31-84

During the calendar year 19____, I paid more than 10% of the support of _____
(Name of person)
I could have claimed this person as a dependent except that I did not pay more than 50% of his or her support.
I understand that this person is being claimed as a dependent on the income tax return of _____
(Name)

_____
(Address)
I agree not to claim an exception for this person on my Federal income tax return for any tax year beginning in this calendar year.

_____ _____
(Your signature)   (Your social security number)

_____ _____
(Date)   (Address)

For example, you, your brother, and your two aunts provide the entire support for your mentally disabled sister during the year. You provide 45%, your brother 35%, and your two aunts provide 10% each. Either you or your brother may claim an exemption and medical deductions for your sister. If you claim your sister as a dependent, your brother, since he provided more than 10% of the support, must file a written statement on Form 2120. He thereby agrees not to claim your sister as a dependent or to receive an exemption and medical deductions. Neither of the aunts has to file Form 2120 because neither provides over 10% of the dependent's support.

For family tax-planning purposes, the person in the highest tax bracket should claim the disabled person as a dependent and receive the exemption and medical deductions. Since this person will receive the most tax shelter, he or she should pay all the medical bills; and the other people should provide support for nondeductible expenses. Remember, you can deduct only the bills you pay for. The tax money saved by the person in the highest tax bracket can be fairly split among all the people who provide support for the disabled person. However, if you are reimbursed by others who signed the multiple-support agreement, you must reduce your deduction by the amount of reimbursement.

WHAT TYPES OF MEDICAL EXPENSES ARE DEDUCTIBLE?

According to the IRS a medical expense includes "any amount paid for the diagnosis, cure, mitigation, treatment, or prevention of disease, or for the purpose of affecting any structure or function of the body, and transportation cost on a trip primarily for and essential to medical care." It is interesting to note that the IRS definition of medical care is much broader than the definition of medical care for health insurance purposes (as will be discussed in the insurance chapter).

Following is a list of items that you should consider in figuring your medical expense deduction. The items are listed in alphabetical order.

Ambulance. You may include in medical expenses amounts you pay for ambulance service.

Analysis. You may include payments for psychoanalysis. You may not include payments for psychoanalysis that you must get as a part of your training to be a psychoanalyst.

Braille books and magazines. You may include the difference in cost of braille books and magazines over regular books and magazines.

Note: The chart and forms on the next two pages will help determine whether an individual qualifies as a dependent.

Who may qualify as your dependent?

1. If the person was your legally adopted child and lived in your home as a member of your household for the entire tax year, answer "yes" to this question.
2. Answer "yes" to this question if you meet the multiple support requirements under *Multiple Support Agreement.*
3. *If neither the person nor the person's spouse is required to file a return but they file a joint return to claim a refund of tax withheld, you may answer "no" to this question.*

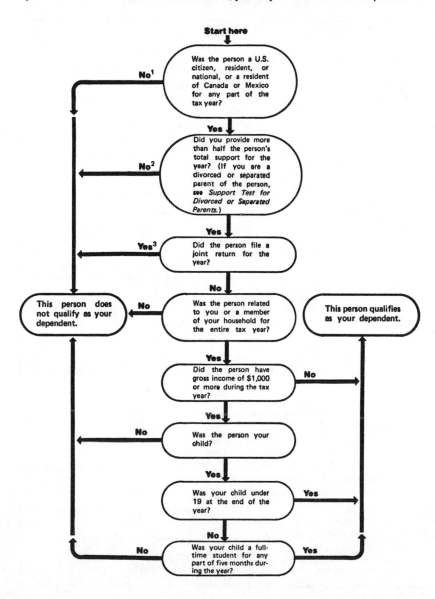

Worksheet for Determining Support

Dependent's Income	1) Did the dependent receive any income, such as wages, interest, dividends, pensions, rents, social security, or welfare? (If yes, complete lines 2, 3, 4, and 5)	☐ Yes ☐ No
	2) Total income received by dependent	$
	3) Amount of dependent's income used for his or her support	$
	4) Amount of dependent's income used for other purposes	$
	5) Amount of dependent's income saved	$
	(The total of lines 3, 4, and 5 should equal line 2)	
Expenses for Entire Household (where dependent lived)	6) Lodging (Complete item a or b)	
	a) Rent paid	$
	b) If not rented, show fair rental value of home. If dependent owns home, include this amount in line 20.	$
	7) Food	$
	8) Utilities (heat, light, water, etc.)	$
	9) Repairs (not included in line 6a or 6b)	$
	10) Other. Do not include expenses of maintaining home, such as mortgage interest, real estate taxes, and insurance.	$
	11) Total household expenses (Add lines 6 through 10)	$
	12) Number of persons, including dependent, living in household	
Expenses for Dependent Only	13) Dependent's part of household expenses (line 11 divided by line 12)	$
	14) Clothing	$
	15) Eduction	$
	16) Medical, dental	$
	17) Travel, recreation	$
	18) Other (specify)	
	19) Total cost of dependent's support for the year (Add lines 13 through 18)	$
	20) Amount dependent provided for own support (line 3, plus line 6b if dependent owns home)	$
	21) Amount others provided for dependent's support. Include amounts provided by state, local and other welfare societies or agencies.	$
	22) Amount you provided for dependent's support (line 19 minus lines 20 and 21)	$
	23) 50% of line 19	$

If line 22 is more than line 23, you meet the support test for the dependent. If the dependent meets the other dependency tests, you may claim an exemption for that person. If line 23 is more than line 22, you may still be able to claim an exemption for the dependent under a multiple support agreement.

Capital expenses. Amounts you pay for special equipment installed in your home or other special improvements that increase the value of the property may be partly deductible as medical expenses. The amount paid for the improvement is reduced by the increase in the value of the property. The rest is deductible medical expense.

Example: Your daughter has a heart ailment. On her doctor's advise, you install an elevator in your home so that she will not have to climb stairs. The elevator costs $2,000. An appraisal shows that the elevator increases the value of your home by $1,400.

You figure your medical deduction as follows: The amount you paid for the improvement ($2,000) minus the increase in value of your home ($1,400) equals your medical expense deduction ($600).

Operation and Upkeep: If a capital expense qualifies as a medical expense, amounts you pay for operation and upkeep also qualify as medical expenses, so long as the medical reason for the capital expense exists. This is so even if you are not allowed to deduct any part of the capital expense because the increase in the value of your home is equal to, or more than, the capital expense.

Example: If, in the previous example, the elevator increased the value of your home by $2,000, you would have no medical deduction for the cost of the elevator. However, the cost of electricity to operate the elevator and repairs to maintain it are deductible so long as the medical reason for the elevator exists.

Improvements To Property Rented By A Handicapped Person: Amounts paid by a handicapped person to buy and install special fixtures in a rented house are medical expenses.

Example: John Smith is handicapped with cerebral palsy and a heart condition. He cannot climb stairs or get into a bathtub. On his doctor's advice, he installs a bathroom with a shower stall on the first floor of his two-story rented house. The landlord did not pay any of the cost and did not lower the rent. John may include in medical expenses the whole amount paid.

Car. *Special Equipment:* You may include in medical expenses the cost of special hand controls and other special equipment installed in a car for the use of a handicapped person.

Special Design: If you have a car designed to hold a wheelchair you may include its costs beyond the cost of a regular car.

Cost of Operation: You may *not* deduct the cost of operating a specially equipped car, except as noted under Transportation.

Crutches. Cost of bought or rented crutches is allowable.

Dancing lessons, swimming lessons, etc. You may *not* deduct the cost of dancing lessons, swimming lessons, etc., even if they are recommended by your doctor for the general improvement of one's health.

Dental fees. You may include in medical expenses the amounts you pay for dental treatment. This includes fees paid to dentists, X-rays, fillings, braces, extractions, and false teeth.

Diaper service. Diaper service is usually not deductible. However, if your disabled child will always wear diapers because of a disability, diaper service is probably deductible.

Doctor's fees. You may include fees you pay to doctors. This includes, but is not limited to, fees to

- chiropodists
- ophthalmologists
- osteopaths
- podiatrists

- psychiatrists
- surgeons
- pediatricians
- dermatologists

- anesthesiologists
- gynecologists
- obstetricians
- neurologists

Psychiatric Care: You may include in medical expenses amounts you pay for psychiatric care. This includes the cost of supporting a mentally ill dependent at a specially equipped medical center where the dependent receives medical care. See Analysis and Transportation.

Eyeglasses. You may include amounts you pay for eyeglasses and contact lenses you need for medical reasons. You may also include fees paid for eye examinations.

Foods, special. You may include in your medicine and drug expenses the cost of special foods or drinks your doctor prescribed to relieve or treat an illness. They must be in addition to your normal diet and not a part of your normal nutritional needs. Do not include the cost of special foods or drinks that replace what you normally eat or drink.

Doctor's Statement: You should attach to your return a statement from your doctor showing that you need the special foods or drinks.

Example 1: Your doctor prescribes 2 ounces of whiskey twice a day for relief of angina pain. The cost of the prescribed amount of whiskey is a deductible medical expense.

Example 2. You have an ulcer and your doctor puts you on a special diet. You may not deduct the cost of your foods or drinks because the special diet replaces what you normally eat or drink.

Funeral expenses. Not deductible.

Guide dog. You may include in medical expenses the cost of a guide dog for the blind or deaf. Amounts you pay for the care of the dog are also medical expenses.

Health Maintenance Organization (HMO). You may include in medical expenses amounts you pay to entitle you to receive medical care from a health maintenance organization. These amounts are treated as medical insurance premiums.

Hearing aids. You may include in medical expenses the cost of a hearing aid and the batteries you buy to operate it.

Hospital services. You may include in medical expenses amounts you pay for hospital services. See Meals.

Household help. You may *not* deduct the cost of household help, even if your doctor recommends it because you are physically unable to do housework. See Nursing services.

Insurance—premiums, policies, and plans. The law has changed in regard to insurance premiums. For tax year 1982, you were allowed to deduct half the amount you paid for medical insurance but not more than $150. The rest was added to your other medical expenses and was subject to the 3% limit.

For tax year 1983, there will no longer be a deduction of up to $150 for half of medical insurance premiums paid. Under the new law, beginning in 1983, you should add all your medical premiums to your other medical expenses and this sum is subject to the new 5% limit, discussed later in the section "How Do I Deduct these Medical Expenses?"

Premiums: Your medical insurance premiums are amounts paid for medical care, whether the payments under the policy are made directly to the provider of the care (hospital, doctor, etc.), the patient, or to you. Do not reduce medical insurance premiums you deduct on your return by any payment you receive from your insurance plan.

You may include premiums you pay for policies that provide payment for

- Hospitalization, surgical fees, X-rays, etc.

- Prescription drugs

- Replacement of lost or damaged contact lenses

- Membership in an association that gives cooperative, or so-called "free-choice" medical service, or group hospitalization and clinical care.

If you have a policy that provides more than one kind of payment, you may deduct the premiums for the medical care part of the policy if the charge for the medical part is reasonable and the cost of that part is separately stated in the insurance contract or given to you in a separate statement.

Medicare B: Medicare B is supplementary medical insurance. Premiums you pay for Medicare B are deductible. Check the information you received from the Social Security Administration.

Medicare A: Medicare A, basic Medicare, is hospital insurance. If you have to pay monthly premiums to get this coverage, you may deduct these premiums. You may *not* deduct Medicare A premiums paid as part of your Social Security tax.

Prepaid Insurance Premiums: You may deduct premiums you pay before you are 65 for insurance for medical care for yourself, your spouse, and your dependents after you reach 65. These premiums are deductible in the year paid if they are

- Payable in equal yearly installments or more often, and

- Paid for at least 10 years, or until you reach age 65, but not for less than 5 years.

Employer Health Plans For Retirees. Under certain employer health plans, you may continue to participate in the plan after you retire. You may either receive a cash payment for your unused sick leave or have the payment applied to the cost of insurance. When you retire under such a plan, you must include the value of the unused sick leave in your gross income. You may deduct the payment applied to the cost of insurance as a medical insurance premium.

If you retire under a health plan that provides that your

employer automatically apply your unused sick leave pay to your health insurance premiums, you do not include the value of the unused sick leave in your gross income. You may not deduct the premiums as a medical expense.

You May Not Include premiums you pay for

- Life insurance policies

- Policies providing payment for loss of earnings

- Policies for loss of life, limb, sight, etc.

- Policies that pay you a guaranteed amount each week for a stated number of weeks if you are hospitalized for sickness or injury.

- The part of your car insurance premiums that provides medical insurance coverage for all persons injured in or by your car.

Lead poisoning. You may include in medical expenses the cost of removing lead-based paints from surfaces in your home to prevent a child who has or had lead poisoning from eating the paint. These surfaces must be in poor repair (peeling or cracking) or within the child's reach. The cost of repainting the scraped area is not a medical expense.

If, instead of removing the paint, you cover the area with wallboard or paneling, you would treat these items as capital expenses. See Capital Expenses. Do not include the cost of painting the wallboard as a medical expense.

Learning disability. Tuition or tutoring fees you pay on your doctor's advice for a child who has severe learning disabilities caused by a nervous disorder may be included in medical expenses.

Legal fees. You may include legal fees paid to allow treatment for mental illness. If part of the legal fees is not for medical care, you may not include that part in medical expenses.

Lifetime care: You may include in medical expenses a life-care fee or "founder's fee" you pay monthly or as a lump sum under an agreement with a retirement home. The amount must be set apart for medical care. The agreement must require a lump-sum payment or advance payment as a condition for the home's promise to provide lifetime care that includes medical care.

Advance Payments: You may include advance payments to a private institution to provide for the lifetime care, treatment, and training of your physically or mentally handicapped dependent when you die or become unable to provide care. The payments must be a condition for the institution's future acceptance of your dependent and must not be refundable in order for you to include them.

Meals. You may include in medical expenses the cost of meals and lodging at a hospital or similiar institution if the main reason for being there is to receive medical care. See Nursing Home.

Do not deduct the cost of meals and lodging while you are away from home for medical treatment, or for the relief of a specific condition, even if the trip is made on the advice of a doctor.

Example: Your dependent son has a heart condition. You live in an area that has cold winters, which makes his condition worse. Your doctor advises your son to spend the winter in a warmer place. You and your family spend the winter in a rented house in Florida. The trip was made for a specific medical reason. None of the expenses for food and rooms while you are on your way to, or while in, Florida are deductible medical expenses. Your son's share of transportation expenses between your home and Florida is deductible. Your and the rest of your family's transportation is not deductible. However, you may include in medical expenses a parent's transporation expenses if a parent must go with the child who needs medical care. It is a question of the age and dependency of the child. See Transportation.

Medical information plan. You may include in medical expenses amounts paid to a plan that keeps your medical information by computer and that can give you the information when you need it. For example, some organizations can store medical information on your disabled child. This information is accumulated while the parents are alive, and is especially helpful for the guardian of the child after the parents die.

Medicines. In tax year 1982 you were able to include in medical expenses amounts you paid for medicines and drugs. They did not have to be prescribed. However, you were not allowed to deduct amounts you spent for items such as—toothpaste, toiletries, cosmetics, and bottled water.

In tax year 1983 you may include in medical expenses *only* prescription drugs and insulin. See the later section on "How Do I Deduct These Medical Expenses?"

Mentally disabled, special home for. You may include in medical expenses the cost of keeping a mentally disabled person in a special home, not the home of a relative, on the recommendation of a psychiatrist to help the person adjust from life in a mental hospital to community living.

Nursing home. You may include the cost of medical care, including meals and lodging, for yourself, your spouse, or your dependents in a nursing home or home for the aged, if the main reason for being there is to get medical care. You may include in medical expenses only the part of the cost that is for medical or nursing care.

Nursing services. Wages and other amounts you pay for nursing services, including an attendant's meals may be included in medical expenses.

Divide the food expenses among the household members to find the cost of the attendant's food. If you had to pay additional amounts for household upkeep because of the attendant, you may deduct the extra amounts. This includes extra rent you pay because you moved to a larger apartment to provide space for the attendant, or the extra cost of utilities for the attendant. If the attendant also provides personal and household services, these amounts must be divided between the time spent in performing household and personal services and the time spent for nursing services. Only the amount spent for nursing services is deductible.

Social Security (FICA) Tax: You may deduct any social security taxes you pay for a nurse, attendant, or other person who provides medical care.

Invalid Spouse: You may include in medical expenses amounts you pay for the care of your invalid spouse in your home. You may deduct only the amounts spent for care to relieve your spouse's illness. You may not deduct the cost of household services, such as cooking and cleaning. See the later section which discusses the credit for household and dependent care expenses.

Healthy Baby: Do not include the cost of nursing services for a normal, healthy baby. But you may be able to take a credit for child care expenses (see later section). You may include in medical expenses amounts you pay for nursing services for an unhealthy baby.

Operations. You may include in medical expenses amounts you pay for legal operations.

Oxygen. The costs you pay for oxygen or oxygen equipment to relieve breathing problems caused by a medical condition may be included.

Psychologist. You may include in medical expenses amounts you pay to a psychologist for medical care.

Schools, special. You may include payments to a special school for a mentally or physically handicapped person if the main reason for using the school is to relieve the handicap. For instance, you may include the cost of a school that

- Teaches braille to a blind child.

- Teaches lipreading to a deaf child.

- Gives remedial language training to correct a condition caused by a birth defect.

The cost of meals, lodging, and ordinary education supplied by a special school may be included in medical expenses only if the main reason for the child's being there is to relieve a mental or physical handicap.

You may not deduct the cost of sending a problem child to a special school for benefits the child may get from the course of study and the disciplinary methods.

Sterilization. You may include in medical expenses the cost of a legally performed operation to make a person unable to have children.

Telephone. You may include the cost and repair of special telephone equipment that lets a deaf person use a regular telephone.

Therapy. You may include in medical expenses amounts you pay for therapy received as medical treatment. For example, payments you make to someone for giving "patterning" exercises are deductible. (These exercises consist mainly of coordinated physical manipulations of the child's arms and legs to imitate crawling and other normal movements.)

Transplants. You may include in medical expenses payments for surgical, hospital, laboratory, and transportation expenses for a donor or a possible donor of a kidney or other transplant.

Transportation. Transportation payments for essential medical care qualify as medical expenses.

You May Include

• Bus, taxi, or plane fare, or ambulance service.

• Actual car expenses, such as gas and oil. Do not include expenses for general repair, maintenance, depreciation, and insurance.

Instead of deducting actual car expenses, you may take 9 cents a mile for each mile you use your car for medical reasons.

• Parking fees and tolls.

• Parent's transportation expenses if a parent must go with a child who needs medical care.

• Transportation expenses of a nurse or other person who can give injections, medications, or other treatment required by a patient who is traveling to get medical care and is unable to travel alone.

• Transportation expenses for regular visits to see a mentally handicapped dependent. These must be recommended as a part of treatment.

• The cost of going to the pharmacist.

You May Not Include

• Transportation expenses to and from work, even if the medical condition requires an unusual means of transportation.

• Transportation expenses if, for nonmedical reasons only, you choose to travel to another city, such as a resort area, for an operation or other medical care prescribed by your doctor.

Trips. You may *not* include in medical expenses a trip or vacation taken for a change in environment, improvement of morale, or general improvement of health, even if the trip was made on the advice of a doctor.

Tuition fees. You may include charges for medical care that are included in the tuition fee of a college or private school if the charges are separately stated in the bill, or given to you by the school.

Weight loss program. You may *not* deduct the cost of a weight loss program even if a doctor advises the program for general health.

Wheelchair. You may include in medical expenses amounts you pay for an autoette or a manual or motorized wheelchair used mainly for the relief of sickness or disability, and not just to provide transportation to and from work. The cost of operating and keeping up the autoette or wheelchair is also a deductible medical expense.

Workshops. If you are a parent of a handicapped child, your doctor may advise you to attend meetings of groups of other parents of handicapped children. It might be a good idea to have a letter from your doctor on record. The cost of these meetings, including transportation or any other doctor recommended activity, may also be considered a deductible expense. For example, your doctor may recommend that you attend a meeting for parents of handicapped children which is a workshop for handling your child's handicap. The cost of the workshop is $100. You may add this $100 expense to your other medical expenses.

X-ray fees. You may include in medical expenses amounts you pay for X-rays.

Payments received for medical expenses. You must reduce your total medical expenses for the year by the payments (reimbursements) received from insurance or other sources for those expenses during the year. This includes payments from Medicare.

Medicine And Drug Expense Reimbursement: Medicine and drug expenses must be reduced by any reimbursements received for them.

Accident Insurance: You must reduce your medical expenses by the part of the payment you get from an accident insurance policy that is for hospitalization and medical care. Do not reduce medical expenses by any payment you receive for loss of earnings or damages for personal injury.

If you pay the entire premium for your medical insurance or all the costs of a similar plan and you receive from the insurance company or similar plan a payment equal to, or more than, your medical expense for the year, you do not have a medical deduction. The amount of the reimbursement you receive that is more than your medical expense is excess reimbursement. Do not include excess reimbursement in your gross income.

Premiums Paid By You And Your Employer: As will be discussed in the insurance chapter, it is often easiest to get medical insurance for your handicapped child and family through a company policy. If you and your employer both contribute to your medical plan, and you receive an excess reimbursement, include in your gross income the part of your excess reimbursement that is from your employer's contribution.

Example: You are covered by a medical insurance policy paid for partly by contributions from your wages. Your gross income does not include the amounts paid by your employer. The annual policy premium is $480. Your employer pays $160 of that amount and the balance of $320 is taken out of your wages. The part of any excess reimbursement you received under the policy that is from your employer's contributions is figured like this:

Total cost of policy	$480
Amount paid by employer	$160
Employer's contribution in relation to the total annual cost of the policy ($160 ÷ $480)	1/3

You must include in your gross income one-third of the excess reimbursement you received for medical expenses under the policy.

Premiums Paid By Your Employer: If your employer paid the total cost of your medical insurance plan and your employer's contributions are not included in your gross income, include all of your excess reimbursement in your gross income.

More Than One Policy: If you are covered under more than one policy, the costs of which are paid by both you and your employer, you must divide the costs to figure the part of any excess reimbursement that is from your employer's contribution.

Example: You are covered by your employer's health insurance policy. The annual premium is $240. Your employer pays $90 and the balance of $150 is deducted from your wages. You also paid the whole premium ($120) for a personal health insurance policy.

During the year you paid medical expenses of $900. In the same year, you were reimbursed $700 under your employer's policy and $500 under your personal policy.

You figure the part of any excess reimbursement you receive that is from your employer's contribution like this:

Reimbursement from employer's policy	$700
Reimbursement from your policy	$500
Total Reimbursement	$1,200

Amount of medical expenses from your policy ($500 ÷ $1,200) × $900 of total medical expenses)	$375
Amount of medical expenses from your employer's policy ($700 ÷ $1,200) × $900 of total medical expenses)	$525
Total Medical Expenses	$900
Excess Reimbursement From Your Employer's Policy ($700-$525)	$175

Because both you and your employer contributed to the cost of this policy, you must divide the cost again to determine the excess reimbursement from your employer's contribution.

Employer's contribution in relation to the annual cost of the policy ($90 ÷ $240)	3/8

You must include in your gross income three-eighths of the excess reimbursement of $175, or $65.62.

HOW DO I DEDUCT THESE MEDICAL EXPENSES?

The laws in regard to how you compute your medical deductions have changed. The easiest way to explain these changes is to illustrate what the law was for the taxable year 1982 and the changes for tax years 1983 and 1984.

For tax year 1982 you were able to deduct only the amount of your medical expenses that was more than 3% of your adjusted gross income. For example, your adjusted gross income was $20,000—3% of which is $600. You paid medical expenses of $700 in 1982. You may deduct $100 for medical expenses. Note the term "3% limit" will be used to refer to 3% of your adjusted gross income. The phrase "subject to the 3% limit" will mean that you must subtract 3% of your adjusted gross income from your medical expenses.

For tax year 1982, you were able to deduct half the amount you paid for medical insurance premiums, but not more than $150. The amount you paid above the $150 was added to your other medical expenses, subject to the 3% limit. For example, if you paid medical insurance premiums of $350 for the year, you could deduct a flat $150 and add $200 to your other medical expenses, which would be subject to the 3% limit.

For tax year 1982, your medicine and drug expenses were subject to the 3% limit and a 1% limit. You added the costs for medicines, both prescription and non-prescription, which exceeded

1% of your adjusted gross income to your other medical expenses, which were then subject to the 3% limit. For example, your adjusted gross income is $12,000. You paid $220 for medicines and drugs in 1981. 1% of your adjusted gross income was $120, so you were allowed to add $100 to your other medical expenses, which were subject to the 3% limit.

Beginning in tax year 1983, you may deduct medical expenses only above 5% of your adjusted gross income. For example, if your adjusted gross income is $20,000 you can deduct only medical expenses in excess of 5% of $20,000 or $1,000. Whereas, for your taxable 1982 year if your adjusted gross income was $20,000 you could deduct medical expenses in excess of 3% of $20,000 or $600. Obviously, this change in the law hurts taxpayers.

The second tax change beginning in taxable year 1983 affects medical insurance premiums. There will no longer be a flat $150 deduction for insurance premiums paid. For taxable year 1983 you can include all medical insurance premiums with your other medical expenses subject to the 5% limit.

The third tax change takes effect for the taxable year 1984, a year after the other tax changes occur. Beginning in 1984 the 1% limitation on medicines will be repealed and all spending on drugs will be added to your other medical expenses and deductible if they exceed 5% of your adjusted gross income. However, for tax year 1984 only drugs prescribed by your doctor and insulin will be eligible expenses. Non-prescription drugs will no longer be eligible for deduction.

Since for tax year 1983 you may deduct only the amount of your medical bills that exceeds 5% of your adjusted gross income, you may have the exasperating experience of falling just short of the deductible level year after year. In this case, try to accelerate or postpone payments so they fall into a year when your medical payments exceed that "magic number." For example, if your adjusted gross income in a given year is $12,000, only medical payments in excess of $600 (5%) may be deducted. Therefore, if in December of a given year, you have accumulated medical expenses of $500 for the year and expect another $500 in January, try to accelerate the January payment to December. This way you have a $400 medical deduction in one year rather than having no deduction in either year. Remember, a limited deduction is allowed to every individual for expenses *paid* during the taxable year for medical care for the taxpayer, the spouse, or a dependent of the taxpayer.

CHILD AND DISABLED DEPENDENT CARE CREDIT

If you pay someone to care for a dependent under 15, for a disabled dependent, or for a disabled spouse in order that you can work or look for work, you may be able to take a tax credit for 30% of the amount you pay. You can use Form 2441, Credit for Child and Dependent Care Expenses, to figure your credit. You may use up to $2,400 of these expenses if you have one qualifying dependent and up to $4,800 if you have two or more qualifying dependents. Your credit cannot be more than 30% of your expenses. See Limits on Work-Related Expenses, discussed later. To qualify for the credit

1. You must file Form 1040, not Form 1040A,

2. Your child and dependent care expenses must be for the purpose of allowing you to work or look for work,

3. You must have income from work during the year,

4. You must keep up a home that you live in with one or more qualifying persons, and

5. You must pay someone other than a child of yours who is under 19 or a person you can claim as your dependent.

Work requirement. Your work can be for others, full time or part time, or in your own business or partnership. Work may include actively looking for work. Unpaid volunteer work or work for a nominal salary does not qualify.

If you are married and you want to qualify for this tax credit, you must file a joint return, unless you are living apart. Both of you must work. If you work and your spouse does not, your spouse is treated as working and earning income during any month the rules in the next paragraph are met.

Student-spouse or spouse not able to care for himself or herself. Your spouse is considered to have worked if

1. He or she was a full-time student during each of 5 months during the tax year, or

2. He or she was physically or mentally not able to care for himself or herself.

Figure the earned income of the non-working spouse as shown under Earned Income Limit, in a later section.

Keeping up a home. You are keeping up a home if you (and your spouse if you are married) pay more than half the cost of running it. Your home means your principal home. It must be your home as well as the home of a qualifying person. A qualifying person's temporary absence will not stop your home from being the person's principal home.

Upkeep expenses normally include property taxes, mortgage interest, rent, utility charges, home repairs, insurance on the home, and food eaten at home.

Do not include as upkeep any payments for clothing, education, medical treatment, vacations, life insurance, transportation, mortgage principal, or for the purchase, improvement, or replacement of property. For example, the cost of replacing a water heater is not considered upkeep, but the cost of repairing a water heater can be included.

Such payments as *Aid to Families with Dependent Children (AFDC)* received from the state that you use to keep up your home are considered to be provided by the state, not by you. If you do not provide more than half the cost of keeping up your home from your own funds, you cannot claim the child and dependent care credit.

Qualifying persons. Your work-related expenses must be for the care of one or more members of your home who are qualifying persons. A qualifying person is

1. A dependent under 15 for whom you can claim a personal exemption deduction, or

2. Either a dependent, or a person you could claim as a dependent except that he or she has a gross income of $1,000 or more, who is not able to care for himself or herself, or

3. Your spouse who is physically or mentally not able to care for himself or herself.

Physical or mental incapacity must be disabling. Persons who are not able to dress, clean, or feed themselves because of physical or mental problems are not able to care for themselves. Persons with mental defects who require constant attention to prevent them from injuring themselves or others are considered not able to care for themselves.

Child of divorced or separated parents. If you are divorced, legally separated under a decree of divorce or separate mainte- nance, or separated under a written separation agreement, your child qualifies if you had custody for a longer time during the calendar year than the other parent. The child does not have to be your dependent, but your child must

1. Be under 15, or not able to care for himself or herself,

2. Be in the custody of one or both parents for more than half of the year, and

3. Receive more than half support from one or both parents.

Work-related expenses. Only work-related expenses qualify for the credit. Your expenses must have been for the well-being and protection of a qualifying person. They are considered to be work related if they allowed you (and your spouse, if married) to work. Expenses are not considered work related merely because you have them while you were working. Whether you had the expenses to allow you to work depends on the facts. You must have paid the expenses to care for one or more qualifying persons, or for household services if part of the services was for the care of qualifying persons. You do not have to choose the least expensive manner of providing care. Work related expenses may include home expenses, child care expenses, disabled dependent care expenses, and disabled spouse care expenses.

Home expenses you pay for ordinary services done in and around your home that were necessary to run your home are included if they were partly for the well-being and protection of a qualifying person. The services of a housekeeper, maid, or cook are usually considered necessary to run your home if performed at least partly for the benefit of the qualifying person. Chauffeur or gardener costs are not. Do not include expenses of food, clothing, education, or entertainment for the qualifying person.

Your expenses may include work-related expenses for household services or for the care of a qualifying person as other unrelated purposes. Your work-related expense is only for the costs of household services or care. You will have to make a reasonable allocation. You do not have to make an allocation if the expense for the unrelated purpose is a small part of the total cost. All of your expenses for household work are work related even if only part of them is for a qualifying person.

If your housekeeper ate in your home, add to your care expenses the part of your total food cost that was for the housekeeper. If you had extra expenses for lodging for your housekeeper, you may add these expenses to your care expenses. For example, if you moved to an apartment with an extra bedroom for the housekeeper, you may include the extra rent and utility expenses for this bedroom. You may not include as care expenses amounts you pay a housekeeper for home and dependent care expenses while you are off work because of illness.

Child care expenses are not limited to services performed in your home. You may include expenses for nursery school or day care for preschool children if they attended in order to allow you to work. Amounts you paid for food, clothing, or schooling are not child care expenses. However, if a nursery school or day-care center provides lunch and educational services as a part of their preschool child care services, treat the entire cost as child care. Do not treat schooling in the first grade or higher as a part of child care. You must divide the total cost between the cost of caring for the child and the cost of schooling.

The cost of getting the child to and from your home and the care location is *not* considered a child care expense. This includes the cost of getting your child to the care location by bus, subway, taxi, or private car.

Disabled dependent or disabled spouse care expenses.
Work-related expenses for a disabled dependent or spouse, who lives in your home at least 8 hours a day, will include services performed in your home to allow you to work and will also include expenses for out-of-home care. If out-of-home care is furnished by a dependent care center, the center must comply with state and local laws. A dependent care center is a facility that furnishes care for more than 6 people, other than people who live at the center, and that receives a fee, payment, or grant for furnishing the care.

Payments to relatives. When figuring your credit, you may not use payments you made to your dependent or your child if he or she was under 19 at the end of the year. You may use payments you made to relatives who are not your dependents, even if they lived in your home.

Limits on work-related expenses. There are limits on the amount of work-related expenses you may take to figure the credit. These include both an *earned income limit* and a *dollar limit.*

Earned income limit. During any tax year, the amount of work-related expenses that you may use to figure your credit may not be more than

1. Your earned income for the year, if you are single at the end of your tax year, or

2. Your earned income or the earned income of your spouse, whichever is less, for the year, if you are married at the end of your tax year.

If you are married and, for any month, your spouse is either a full-time student or not able to care for himself or herself, your spouse will be considered to have earned income of $200 a month if there is one qualifying person in your home, or $400 a month if there are two or more qualifying persons in your home. A spouse who cannot care for himself or herself is a qualifying person.

Dollar limit. You may be able to take a tax credit of as much as 30% of work-related expenses if your adjusted gross income is $10,000 or less. The 30% is reduced by one percent for each $2,000 or part of $2,000 of adjusted gross income above $10,000 until the percentage is reduced to 20% for income above $28,000. The limit on work-related expenses is $2,400 for one qualifying person and $4,800 for two or more persons.

For example, a widower pays a housekeeper $5,000 a year to take care of his home and his disabled daughter while he is working. He earns $20,000 during the year. Since there is only one qualifying person, the daughter, the maximum work-related expenses he can claim are $2,400, even though he spent at least $5,000. Therefore, the largest credit he can claim is 25% of $2,400 or $600. The 25% credit is calculated by reducing the 30% credit by one percent for every $2,000 of income above $10,000. Since the widower had income of $20,000, the 30% credit is reduced by 5%.

Marital status. If you are married at the end of your tax year, you must file a joint return with your spouse to qualify for the credit. If you are legally separated from your spouse under a decree of divorce or of separate maintenance, you are not considered married. You may claim the credit on a separate return. If you are married and file a separate return, you will not be considered married if

1. Your home was the home of a qualifying person for more than half the tax year,

2. You paid more than half the cost of keeping up your home for the tax year, and

3. Your spouse did not live in your home for the last 6 months of the tax year.

How to claim credit. To claim the credit, you must file your return on Form 1040. You should complete Form 2441, Credit for Child and Dependent Care Expenses, or a statement showing how you figured the credit, and send it in with your Form 1040.

Medical expenses. Some disabled dependent care expenses may qualify as work-related and also as medical expenses. You *cannot* use the same expenses to give you both a credit and a medical expense deduction. If these expenses are more than you can use to figure your credit, because of the *earned income limit* or the *dollar limit,* discussed earlier, you may add the excess to your medical expenses before subtracting the 5% limit. However, if you use them first in calculating your medical expenses, you cannot use any part of them to figure your work-related expense.

TAX PREPARERS

Now you should realize there are many medical deductions and credits available to families of the handicapped. If you are uncertain about whether an expense qualifies as a deduction or about your taxes in general, there are many sources of assistance available. You should look for tax help early in the tax year. Select a tax professional by reference from friends and professionals. Once you find someone to help you with your taxes, agree to a general fee before hiring. And, although your tax preparer should sign your tax return, make sure you understand everything that is written on it because you are responsible for any errors.

In addition to tax services, three useful tax guides exist: *Your Federal Income Tax*, available for 75 cents from IRS offices or the Superintendent of Documents, Washington, D.C.; *The Master Tax Guide* published by Commerce Clearance House and available at most libraries; J.K. Lasser's *Your Income Tax*, available at book stores for $5.95.

The following list describes different types of services available that will either prepare your return for you or help you fill it out.

Internal revenue service. The IRS provides many services at no charge. First, you can call the IRS on a toll-free number, available from your local IRS office, to get answers to specific questions. There is also a new service for those with push-button phones. This service, called TeleTax, offers recorded messages of basic tax information. To use the recorded-message system you dial the TeleTax number and then follow instructions. Each tape has a different 3 digit tape number: For example: Dependent: who can be claimed? Tape 325. Itemized deductions: Tape 423. For more information on how to use TeleTax ask the IRS for publication 910.

Second, you can walk into any IRS office for free tax help. The problem with this free help is that the IRS staff is usually very busy and can spend little time in computing, let alone planning, your taxes. Normally, you will be one of a group being helped by an IRS employee. *Only the handicapped* receive one-on-one assistance. In general, seek help at a local IRS office only if your financial situation is not complex. If you seek IRS help, by the way, the IRS cannot ask you to substantiate your deductions. For these visits, they are there to help, not to audit.

Third, the IRS has a program called Outreach in which the agency will go into communities to offer help, sometimes in cooperation with local organizations.

Telephone help for deaf or hearing-impaired taxpayers is available for those who have access to TV/Telephone-TTY equipment. Residents of Indiana should call 1-800-382-4059. Residents of all other states call 1-800-428-4732. Braille materials are made available through the IRS for distribution through the Library of Congress.

Other free assistance. Several organizations offer free help in preparing tax returns. One such program is called the Tax Aide/Tax Counseling for the Elderly, run by the American Association of Retired Persons (AARP) for anyone at least 60 years old. Volunteers, many of whom are retired accountants or businessmen, are trained by the IRS and the Association to give one-on-one help to the elderly. For more information, call the IRS after Feb. 1 in any year.

Another free service is called the Volunteer Income Tax Assistance Program, or VITA. Groups from colleges, community associations, and other organizations are trained by the IRS to provide help in their own communities for those with relatively uncomplicated tax returns. For further information, watch for publicity in your area or call the IRS.

Commercial preparers. These services, such as H&R Block, are convenient, relatively inexpensive, and competent to handle the not-too-complicated tax return. Commercial preparers fill out tax returns, but they do not plan your taxes on an on-going basis.

National tax services like H&R Block usually offer two guarantees. First, they guarantee to pay interest and penalties you receive as a result of their staff's improperly filling out your tax return. Second, if a client is audited, they will accompany the client free to the audit to explain how the return was filed. You should ask all tax preparers before you hire them whether or not they will extend these guarantees.

National tax services are to be preferred over local tax services. These local tax services often charge more and their staffs often have had less tax training. The only way to judge them is by asking others who have used them.

Enrolled agents. These tax preparers have passed an IRS examination and received what is known as a "Treasury Card," which means their background has been checked. Enrolled agents will represent you before the IRS except in court. Most enrolled agents are hired b·y people who expect to be audited or who have complicated returns.

Usually, enrolled agents charge higher fees than commercial preparers but lower fees than accountants or lawyers. An enrolled agent would probably charge a minimum of $40 to $50 for a simple single return. More complicated returns might cost approximately $50 for each hour worked on them.

Accountants. As your income becomes greater and your tax return more complicated, you should consider hiring an accountant. An accountant deals with taxes regularly and can help you plan your taxes throughout the year. Usually, it is better to hire a certified public accountant (CPA) than a regular accountant, because CPAs are college graduates who also have passed a comprehensive accounting exam. CPAs will represent their client before the IRS except in court.

Inquire about the type of client the CPA most often handles. From this information, you can determine whether his or her specialty meets your needs—individual tax planning, small business accounting, professional corporations, or whatever.

Accountants usually charge relatively high fees for tax preparation. A minimum fee might be $100. An accountant usually charges around $50 an hour. So it pays to have well organized tax records. If you have a complicated return, especially for families with disabled dependents, it may be worth the extra fees to have your taxes figured correctly. An accountant will probably save you money even with the high charge and you will feel more secure that you have done it correctly.

Tax attorneys. Generally, tax attorneys deal with the most complicated tax questions. Tax attorneys will often handle tax shelters for wealthy individuals, corporate returns, tax forms concerning estates and trusts, or business deals that have tax ramifications. The tax attorney is the only tax preparer who can represent you in court. An attorney may charge between $50 and $175 an hour.

(Note: Much of the information in this chapter and the charts and diagrams are based on IRS Publication 501, 502, 503 and 907. You can obtain these publications and others from your local IRS office.)

Chapter 6
Insurance

The insurance field and its related products have become quite sophisticated. The types of insurance and their functions have increased. For this reason, when purchasing insurance it is important to consult with a good insurance counselor.

Regardless of whether you are purchasing medical or life insurance, carefully read the policy's provisions, and calculate whether the provisions and the amount of the policy satisfy your objectives. Parents of mentally disabled children often need extra insurance because the proceeds must support the disabled person throughout a lifetime. After this analysis, carefully review the choice of beneficiaries. For example, since you may want to avoid giving cash or cash-like assets to your disabled child, the beneficiary of your life insurance policy might be a trust. As discussed in the trust chapter, trusts are particularly useful for families who want to avoid jeopardizing governmental benefits or exposing the disabled person's money to collection by the government.

GENERAL INSURANCE TERMS

This section will explain the various insurance terms you will encounter throughout the chapter.

Annuity. An annuity is a contract designed to pay an income, frequently adjustable for inflation, from a stipulated date for the remaining lifetime of a beneficiary, or for a specified period of time.

Beneficiary. A beneficiary is a person or entity named in the insurance policy who receives the benefits.

Cash value. The term cash value, also known as "surrender" or "loan" value, is most frequently associated with certain types of life insurance policies, usually known as whole life or permanent policies. A portion of the premiums paid on these policies provides for insurance, and the rest adds up over time to form a fund that is available to the owner of the policy as a loan or as an outright cash payment. This is the cash value of the policy. A loan on the policy will decrease the benefit value of the policy by the amount of the loan until it's repaid. An outright payment to the owner of all the accumulated cash will terminate the policy if it's not repaid.

Endowment insurance. Endowment insurance is similar to an annuity investment. The insurance company agrees to pay proceeds at a specified time even if the insured is alive. If the insured dies before this time, the insurance company will pay the beneficiary.

Grace period. A grace period is that period of time, often 31 days, beyond the premium due date that the policy will remain in force. Usually no interest is charged if a premium payment is made during the grace period.

Group medical policy. A group medical policy insures a group of people. Often employee groups are insured by their employer. Under group policies, the insurance company cannot scrutinize the individual applicant as closely as with an individual policy; usually the insured is not required to take a medical examination. Under a group policy, parents can easily obtain medical insurance for the mentally disabled child. Usually, the insured person has the right to convert automatically to an individual policy when he or she leaves the group.

Individual medical policy. An individual medical policy insures an individual rather than a group of individuals. The insurance company may scrutinize the applicant more closely; a medical examination is usually required before the policy is issued.

Premiums. Premiums are the amount of money paid by the insured to the insurance company to obtain insurance protection.

Permanent life insurance. Permanent or whole life insurance, unlike term insurance, covers the insured for an entire lifetime. This coverage is paid at a flat rate annually ("ordinary life" or "straight life insurance") until the death of the insured or over a limited period, say 10 or 20 years ("limited payment insurance").

Permanent life insurance, although more expensive than term insurance, provides many options. A permanent policy builds up its own "net worth" or cash value in two ways. First, the premium payments you make when young are in excess of the cost of insurance protection which pays for your protection in later years. Second, the insurance company earns income on this excess money. This cash value can be borrowed from the insurance company often at much lower than current interest rates. If the insured fails to pay back the borrowed cash value, the insurance company will deduct the amount of the loan and interest from the proceeds of the policy. Some insurance companies pay the insured interest on the cash value of the policy.

Permanent life insurance assures parents of the mentally disabled that they will always be insured. Moreover, premiums for whole life can be a flat rate that will not increase as the insured gets older. This is especially important during the retirement years, when people are often living on a fixed income.

Term insurance Term insurance covers the insured for a set period of time—five years, ten years, or longer. Term insurance is considered as the least expensive, "no-frills" type policy. The expense of the policy depends on your current age and health.

Term insurance will pay the benefits to the beneficiary only if the insured dies during the term of coverage. What if you become seriously ill just as your coverage expires? You would be unlikely to qualify medically for a new policy. To avoid this problem, you should pay extra to include a guaranteed renewable option.

Term insurance is a good option for young parents in good health with relatively low incomes. However, as your age increases each new term becomes more expensive. Eventually, when you reach your sixties, the premiums for term insurance are prohibitively expensive. To avoid this problem, you can purchase convertible term insurance, which gives you the choice of converting to a permanent type of insurance up until a stated age (such as 65), without presenting evidence about your health.

Term insurance, unlike permanent insurance, does not build up a cash value. The cash value in permanent life policies can be borrowed. Term insurance, unlike permanent insurance, does not allow the insured to stop paying insurance premiums and still be insured for a reduced rate.

Waiver of premium. If there is a waiver of premium clause in your policy, a company will not require the payment of premiums during the total disability of the insured. In other words, you will not have to make insurance payments while you are disabled.

MEDICAL INSURANCE FOR MENTALLY DISABLED PEOPLE

Everyone needs medical insurance, particularly disabled people who frequently need medical attention. Because obtaining medical coverage for the mentally disabled can be difficult, families should seek coverage aggressively.

What types of services does medical insurance cover? Parents of mentally disabled children should ask themselves: Does my child need medical insurance? If so, what types of medical services should it cover? How much? How can we obtain medical coverage? If your child already has medical insurance, the same questions can be used to review the current coverage.

Parents of the mentally disabled cannot accept medical insurance at face value. Every medical policy pays for different health services. Parents must analyze and predict the current and future medical needs of their child and choose a plan to cover these needs.

Typically, medical insurance covers only those services provided by a licensed physician or any medical service that takes place in a hospital. This strict definition of medical service creates enormous complications for parents whose mentally disabled child receives medical attention by someone other than a licensed physician (a psychologist, a family counselor, a vocational rehabilitation expert, a social worker) or who receives medical attention at a place other than a hospital (an outpatient program, a mental health center, an intermediate care facility).

Given this strict definition of medical service, parents must weigh many factors to maximize insurance benefits. For instance, should you pay for a less expensive psychologist whose bills are not covered by insurance or pay for a more expensive psychiatrist whose bills are partially covered by your medical insurance? Your disabled child needs only outpatient services and these are not covered; should you hospitalize him or her to obtain insurance coverage? (Outpatient services might be insured if supervised by a licensed physician.) Your insurance policy has a large $500 deductible; should you pay this deductible and have a psychiatrist treat your child, or will the $500 cover treatment with a less expensive psychologist? (Many insurance companies, such as Prudential and Aetna, are beginning to cover clinical psychologists, especially if you request such coverage.) You must carefully analyze the policy's definition of "hospital" and "physician" to determine what types of medical services will be covered by the insurance.

When considering a policy, find out the length of time your disabled child can be covered in a hospital. Period of coverage can vary according to the type of hospital. For instance, in a medical hospital the coverage might be unlimited, whereas in a mental hospital the coverage may be for 30-60 days. You must consider whether you should have your child's mental illness treated in a general hospital, rather than in a mental hospital, to cover long periods of treatment. Is the general hospital competent to treat the mental illness?

Additional coverage particulars to check into include

• Whether the insurance covers custodial care costs. Medical insurance rarely covers the costs of the everyday support received at a residential facility.

• Whether medicine and drugs are covered, partially or totally. If they are not covered, try to buy generic drugs which contain the same ingredients as branded drugs, but are less expensive.

• What types of drugs the policy will pay for.

• Whether it covers psychological diagnostic testing.

• Whether it will pay for the costs of a private home nurse.

As you can see, parents of the mentally disabled cannot rest assured because they have "medical insurance."

How can I obtain medical insurance for my mentally disabled child? *Individual coverage:* Individual medical insurance is difficult to obtain for the mentally disabled child because the insurance company in calculating its risk will inquire about the health and earning power of the mentally disabled person. The insurance companies know mental illnesses are full of uncertainties.

Often, insurance companies will not grant individual coverage to those people who are not self-supporting, unless they are in school or receiving job training. If the insurance company insures the disabled person, the premiums will be determined by the degree and the type of disability.

If you feel the insurance company is taking advantage of you by charging too much for coverage, have a lawyer check your state's insurance code. Some states forbid insurers from discriminating between individuals "of the same class" in premiums for health insurance. Arguably, this could apply to a mentally disabled person if the insurance company has no proof of higher costs associated with the group. Inform the insurance company of your rights under your state's insurance laws (after checking with your lawyer).

The Association for Retarded Citizens (ARC), offers "Supplemental In-Hospital" medical insurance to families with mentally disabled relatives underwritten by the Insurance Company of North America. This medical insurance will supplement your current medical insurance. To be eligible for Supplemental In-Hospital Insurance, the applicant must be a member of ARC and under the age of 60. This insurance can apply to the ARC member, the spouse, and any children. The applicant should remain an ARC member to avoid rate increases and coverage cancellation.

For every day the insured is in the hospital he or she will directly receive supplemental cash payments up to 500 days for each period of hospitalization. The applicant can apply for the $50, $75, or $100 a day in-hospital cash benefits. In addition, handicapped persons may receive a 10% benefit increase for each day of hospitalization up to a maximum of $200 extra per calendar year. For example, if a $100 per day plan were chosen, the insured would receive a 10% bonus. This 10% bonus would increase the daily payments from $100 to $110 up to 20 days. The bonus would expire after 20 days due to the $200 maximum. After the $200 maximum is reached, the insured receives $100 per day.

Benefits begin the first day of hospitalization and continue for up to 500 days of each eligible period of hospitalization. Hospitalization does not include admission

- To an institution owned or operated by any national or state governmental agency.

- To an intermediate care facility for the mentally retarded.

- For pregnancy.

- For a self-inflicted injury.

- For hospital confinement caused by an act of war.

These cash benefits paid to the insured can be used for any purpose, not just hospital costs. To obtain more details concerning the ARC Supplemental In-Hospital insurance, the toll free number is 800-621-9903 or write to

National Association For Retarded Citizens
Group Insurance Administrator
180 N. LaSalle Street
Suite 3220
Chicago, Illinois 60601.

Group insurance coverage: Group insurance is the easiest way to obtain medical insurance for your disabled child. Often, under a large group program coverage is granted without inquiring into the medical history of the insured, because the risks of the insurance company are spread across the entire group. Usually, group medical insurance is obtained in one of two ways: if the disabled person is the dependent of a working parent who is covered under a group plan, or if the disabled person is employed by an organization that offers group medical insurance.

When the disabled person is a dependent of a working parent who is covered under a group plan, usually the medical insurance will extend to the entire family. The group plan extends to dependents of the working family and the policy will define the meaning of the word "dependent." Usually, "dependent" is defined as a child of the working parent who is under a certain age, unmarried, and unable to support himself or herself. According to most definitions of dependent, a severely handicapped person will qualify as a dependent and can remain insured until any age. However, some policies will require that if you have a permanently disabled child you must notify the insurance company, generally when the dependent reaches the age of 19. If you fail to notify the insurance company within a certain time period you might lose the coverage for your dependent child. Some states require that if a dependent child is insured under a group plan and becomes permanently disabled and dependent before the age of 19, the group insurance coverage must be extended to the dependent even after the age of 19. However, under most laws the insurance company must be notified before the dependent reaches 19 years of age. Some state laws allow a 31-day grace period.

What happens when the working parent retires and the group coverage ends? Read the policy or contact someone in the organization responsible for insurance matters and inquire whether you and your dependents can convert to individual coverage without an examination. If not, check your state's insurance laws.

LIFE INSURANCE PLANS FOR PARENTS

Parents can buy life insurance from many insurance companies. However, two life insurance plans have been created especially for parents with mentally disabled children. These plans recognize that parents of the mentally disabled need life insurance to care for the disabled person. Moreover, one of the plans, the Bridge Foundation plan, attempts to combine both life insurance and a personal care plan for the disabled person after the parent's death.

The ARC Protection Plan. The ARC Protection plan is available to any member of a local or state Association for Retarded Citizens (ARC) whose age is between 19 and 65. The purpose of the plan is to provide low-cost insurance through the mass purchasing power of the large ARC membership. You should compare the ARC Protection Plan with other life insurance prices.

An ARC member may apply for one of five amounts of coverage: $10,000, $20,000, $30,000, $40,000 and $50,000. The spouse of a member may also apply at the same time for $5,000 coverage. If both a husband and a wife are ARC members, each may apply for amounts between $10,000 and $50,000.

The amount of the premiums depends upon the age of the insured. The premium costs increase every fifth year. Premiums can be paid annually, semi-annually, and quarterly. Premiums are slightly reduced for annual and semi-annual payments.

The plan contains provisions for converting part or all of the coverage to a whole life plan of insurance. Information about the ARC Protection Plan can be obtained from your local ARC unit or by writing:

ARC Protection Plan
P.O. Box 18384
Tampa, Florida 33679.

The Bridge Foundation. The Bridge Foundation is a new concept in life insurance for parents of the mentally disabled. Since the program is new, you will want to check it out thoroughly. Through the Bridge Foundation parents make tax-deductible monthly contributions (premiums) to the Foundation, and the Foundation contractually guarantees to pay, up to $50,000 annually for the lifetime care of the child after the parents' death. The highlights of the plan are as follows:

• The Bridge Foundation, a non-profit organization, was created to resolve uncertainty when the providing parent of a dependent disabled child dies.

• It was developed by the Mutual Benefit Life Insurance Company, Newark, New Jersey. This insurance company is the fourth oldest in the U.S. and ranks 15th largest in terms of assets.

• The administration costs of the Foundation are paid by the reapportionment of the commissions earned from the sale of the life insurance policies. Therefore, all the monies going into the Foundation benefit disabled people.

• The parent makes tax-deductible contributions to the Bridge Foundation. These contributions buy a $250,000 permanent life insurance policy on the parent's life. The contributions are tax deductible as medical expenses under Revenue Ruling #75-303. (Revenue Rulings, it should be noted, are subject to change.)

The monthly contributions required are:

Age of Insured	Tax Deductible Monthly Contributions
30	$265
35	$322
40	$397
45	$502
50	$642
55	$832

• The Foundation owns the life insurance policy you buy.

• When the parent dies, the Foundation receives the insurance proceeds and is legally obligated to pay up to $50,000 per year to a private residential facility for the lifetime of the child after the death of the parent.

• The Foundation, along with the guardian of your child, will monitor the residential facility in which your child lives. If the facility does not fulfill the needs of your child, another facility will be selected by the guardian and paid by the Foundation.

• If the parent stops contributions to the Foundation, the cash value of the policy remains with the Foundation. However, the insurance policy provides that if the parent cannot earn more than

25% of his or her normal income for a period of four months, the contributions are waived for as long as the income is reduced, and the insurance policy remains in full force.

LIFE INSURANCE TRUSTS

Trusts, in general, are the most useful estate planning tools for families with mentally disabled children. Life insurance trusts and regular trusts function in the same way. As described in the trust chapter, trusts have numerous benefits.

The insurance proceeds that a disabled person receives from his or her parent's policy will cause the identical problems of direct inheritance discussed in the previous chapters:

1. The mentally disabled person might not be able to manage the money.

2. The proceeds may reduce or terminate governmental benefits.

3. The government might bill the disabled person for current and past services.

4. A guardian of the estate might be required to manage the money.

To avoid these problems, parents can create a life insurance trust. When the parent (the owner-insured of the life insurance policy) dies, the proceeds of the life insurance policy go into the trust which is the beneficiary of the insurance *policy*. The disabled person is the beneficiary of the life insurance *trust*. To prevent the disabled child from directly receiving the insurance proceeds, the parent names the trust, rather than the disabled person, as the beneficiary of the insurance policy.

Parents can create four basic types of life insurance trusts—revocable, irrevocable, funded or unfunded. As with all trusts, parents can combine many individual trust characteristics to custom-fit a trust to their particular estate planning goals.

Revocable life insurance trust. Under a revocable life insurance trust, the parent or policyowner retains control over the insurance policy rather than relinquishing control permanently to the trustee. The insured can use various options in the particular policy, such as borrowing on the cash value of a permanent life policy. Moreover, like any other revocable trust, the creator can alter the terms of the trust, change the trustee, or terminate the trust. This flexibility allows parents of mentally disabled children to react to new situations such as a change in their child's financial needs or a change in the law. Although the creator of the trust retains control, the creator knows if he or she dies, the money will flow into the trust and be managed by a skillful trustee.

Like most revocable trusts, there are no tax advantages. Therefore, the insurance proceeds will be included in the creator's taxable gross estate for federal tax purposes. This tax on the proceeds will reduce the amount of money that goes into the trust. However, by the year 1987 the Economic Recovery Tax Act (ERTA) will exempt the first $600,000 of an estate from federal estate tax.

Irrevocable life insurance trust. Under an irrevocable life insurance trust, the parent-insured must give up ownership and control of the insurance policy, and any other assets in the trust, to the trustee. The creator cannot alter the terms of the trust, change the trustee, or terminate the trust. This lack of control is a tremendous disadvantage to parents with a mentally handicapped child, who must be able to react to changing conditions. As with most irrevocable trusts, however, there can be tax advantages.

Funded life insurance trust. The funded life insurance trust is not only named the beneficiary of the parent's life insurance policy, but it also contains other assets in the trust property. These other assets, such as stocks and bonds, can produce income that the trustee may use to pay the insurance premiums.

Unfunded life insurance trust. The unfunded life insurance trust contains no trust property except the beneficial right to the parent's life insurance proceeds. Upon the parent's death, the proceeds are paid to the trust for the benefit of the disabled person.

LIFE INSURANCE FOR THE MENTALLY DISABLED PERSON

Usually, the mentally disabled person is the beneficiary of a policy rather than the owner-insured of a policy. Most mentally handicapped people do not need life insurance because they usually do not have dependents who need protection. However, the trend in the mental health field in recent years is to encourage the mentally disabled to live as normal a life as possible. Today, and increasingly in the future, the mildly disabled may marry and raise families.

Disabled people who have financial dependents need life insurance.

Although the disabled person supports a spouse and perhaps a family, he or she may still rely on various governmental benefits as supplemental support. In this situation, the disabled person needs a plan for buying life insurance without jeopardizing eligibility for governmental benefits.

If the disabled person purchases permanent life insurance and retains ownership of the policy, the cash surrender value of the policy will be included in the disabled person's net worth for eligibility purposes. (The cash surrender value represents the price for which the insurance policy could be cashed in at any given time.)

To avoid jeopardizing the disabled person's eligibility for aid, many courses of action are available. One way to avoid eligibility problems is for the disabled-insured to purchase term rather than whole life insurance. Since term insurance does not contain a cash surrender value, the disabled person's net worth remains unchanged.

Another way to avoid eligibility problems for those programs that consider the net worth only of the applicant and not the net worth of the applicant and his or her family is for the disabled person, as the insured, to give the policy to the beneficiary, perhaps the spouse or child of the disabled policy-owner. By giving the policy to the beneficiary, the disabled person no longer owns the policy nor has the right to surrender it for its cash value. Therefore, the cash surrender value of the policy cannot be included in the disabled person's net worth for eligibility purposes.

Sometimes the only reason for a disabled person to have life insurance is to pay funeral expenses. A better type of insurance to cover funeral expenses is burial insurance. Burial insurance contains no cash surrender value until after the insured's death. Therefore, it does not affect one's net worth for eligibility purposes.

Chapter 7
Financial Planning

Most of us need to know something about investing, if only to stay ahead of inflation. However, investment information is even more essential for those who need to accumulate money for a dependent relative.

The main purpose of this chapter is to help relatives of disabled persons determine whether they need a financial advisor. It will also provide them with some background information on investment, so they can act intelligently either on their own or with an advisor. While it provides some general background information on investing, it is in no sense to be considered as a guide to all types of investing.

Today, in the face of inflation and high taxes, deposits in a savings account are simply not enough. Everyone, no matter at what income level, can benefit by planning carefully before investing even small sums of money.

In deciding how to invest your money, first think about the factors and objectives that affect your finances. Consider your age, present and potential earning power, number and age of dependents, net worth, tax bracket, and other financial data. Think clearly about your family's housing needs, educational goals, and so forth.

Liquidity is another consideration. How often, and how urgently would you need to draw on your invested money? A "liquid" investment is one that can be quickly and easily converted to cash. Funds invested in a "non-liquid" way are inaccessible to the investor for a specified period of time. For example, if you plan to buy a house soon, you should not invest potential down payment funds in a thirty-month "savings certificate" which cannot, without penalty, be converted to cash for at least thirty months. Instead, you could invest those funds in a highly liquid "money market fund" which gives you the option of withdrawing at any time. On the other hand, if you are planning for your disabled child's more distant future, you might be willing to tie up your money in a long term investment if it provides a better return.

Think about risk. How much can you afford to lose? Generally, the higher the potential return, the greater the risk. While everyone desires a large return, clearly not everyone can afford to take large risks. A young couple with a modest income, a mortgage on a new house, and small children should be more cautious with their money than a single person with higher income and fewer obligations.

Once you have outlined your financial condition and objectives, determined your need for access to your investments, and evaluated the degree of risk you are willing to take, you are ready to explore the options for investing. There's a wide range of investment possibilities to suit the needs of almost any investor.

STOCK MARKET

Many people associate financial planning primarily with investment in the stock market. This is not the only investment source, but it can be used to advantage if the investor has enough money and time to spend at it. A wise stock investor will "diversify"— spread his risk over a variety of stocks. Such a diversified "stock portfolio" lowers the investor's risk because if some stocks decrease in value, others may increase thereby creating an overall profit or at least offsetting losses.

A small investor who can buy only a few stocks and who cannot diversify is disadvantaged. If a particular stock drops in value, the small investor has few other stocks to mask the loss. Small investing in the stock market is rarely profitable enough to justify the long hours that must be spent analyzing stock market trends.

MUTUAL FUNDS

As an alternative to individual market investing, many firms offer "mutual funds" in which people who have similiar investment goals buy shares in an investment company. Fund managers jointly invest the money in the stock or bond markets in order to mutually benefit each shareholder. Because he pools his money with others, the mutual fund investor holds an interest in a diversified portfolio as if he were a large-scale investor. Also, he receives professional fund management often unavailable to small, individual investors.

At any time, a shareholder may redeem (cash-in) all or some of the shares for their current "net asset value" (the amount of the original investment plus or minus the amount the shares have earned or lost). A shareholder may accomplish redemption by simply writing a check against his holdings in the fund. With most funds, such checks must be in amounts of $500 or more. Another way to redeem shares is through a wire redemption service. This service allows the shareholder to call the fund management and have the proceeds wired directly into a checking account.

Stocks held by mutual funds and stocks held by individuals receive identical tax treatment. Profit on the stocks that the fund has held for longer than one year will be taxed to the fund as "long term gains," which have a lower tax rate than profit on a stock that was held for less than one year. In this way the tax advantages of the long term capital gain are passed along to fund investors—even to those who have invested in the fund for less than a year. The investor's dividends on mutual funds, however, are taxed as regular income.

Since there is a wide variety of mutual funds and each operates under different investment policies, an investor can benefit from a fund carefully chosen to fit his financial objectives.

When choosing a mutual fund, base your selection on the past performance of the fund. Also, be sure that the fund manager's investment goals are similiar to your own. This information is available in the prospectus for that fund. In the reference section of most libraries you can find a book called *Investment Companies* (Arthur Wiesenberger Services, New York). This book will provide you with some basic information on specific funds. It will also give addresses where you may write for more information, including a prospectus.

Two examples of different types of mutual funds are growth funds and income funds. Investors in a growth fund are generally looking for long term growth. However, because a growth company's profits will be reinvested to help it expand, the growth fund investor may expect small, if any, dividends over the short run. On the other hand, investors in income funds seek current income, but generally cannot expect much long term increase in their stock prices. In accordance with this goal, managers of income funds buy stocks likely to pay high dividends.

A mutual fund investor's profit depends on the value of the stock held by the fund and the dividends paid. Although investment managers study both factors to ensure wise investments, they cannot guarantee their management performance. There is always some risk of loss. Government security mutual funds provide an exception to this risk. Those who invest in a mutual fund which holds government securities take no risk because the securities held by the fund are backed by the United States Government.

MONEY MARKET FUNDS

Just as mutual fund investors jointly invest in stocks or bonds, money market fund investors pool their dollars to invest in money market instruments such as commercial paper, banker's acceptances, and treasury bills. Because these money market instruments are sold at a minimum face value of $10,000, the small investor cannot take advantage of their high return except by investment in a money market fund.

Most funds require a $1,000 minimum investment. The shareholder need not wait for individual instruments held by the fund to "mature" before providing investment returns to the fundholder. Money may be withdrawn at any time. Investors can easily redeem their shares. Many funds offer wire redemption services and $500 minimum check writing privileges. When interest rates are high, investment in a money market fund provides high returns. For these reasons, money market instruments are very attractive to investors seeking a high return on liquid investments.

BONDS

A bond is a certificate of creditorship that is issued to raise capital.

The issuer pays interest on a bond at specified dates and eventually redeems it at maturity, repaying principal plus interest due. Bonds also may be sold before maturity at their current market value which is determined by prevailing interest rates and the company's credit worthiness. Bonds are usually issued at $1,000 face value each.

With bonds, as with stocks, it is difficult for a small investor to diversify. Diversification is important in reducing overall risk. With bonds backed by the U.S. Government, such diversification is not necessary because there is no risk involved, as long as the government remains solvent. But the higher yielding corporate bonds are only as good as the issuing corporation's ability to repay. Therefore, for relative safety, a small investor interested in corporate bonds may want to consider a corporate bond mutual fund with its diversified holdings. Again, as with the other funds above, you may redeem your shares at any time.

TREASURY BILLS

Treasury bills are short term government obligations. They are sold at less than face value at government auctions. They are available in denominations from $10,000 to $1,000,000 and mature at various intervals from one month to one year after purchase. Treasury bills yield a profit equal to their value at maturity (which is the face value) minus their purchase price. For example, an investor paying $9,000 for a one year $10,000 treasury bill is guaranteed to receive the full $10,000 (approximately an eleven percent return) when he cashes it at maturity one year later.

An investor may buy treasury bills in any of three ways: through a bank, through a government securities dealer, or by personally bidding at the government auctions. Banks and brokers will usually charge the investor a $25 to $50 fee. Treasury bills can be bought directly, by bidding at any Federal Reserve Bank's Monday afternoon auction. The bidding can be accomplished either in person or by mail. Usually, however, only sophisticated investors bid by auction.

By buying a treasury bill, an investor lends the price of the bill to the federal government; the government, in turn, guarantees the investment. Because the investment is risk free, and because no state or local income tax need be paid on interest earned on treasury bills, they provide the investor with unique financial opportunities.

SAVINGS CERTIFICATES OF DEPOSIT

A Savings Certificate of Deposit is an interest-bearing bank receipt payable on a specific future date. Certificate interest rates are set each Tuesday, based on the yield of treasury bills auctioned the day before.

Like treasury bills, Savings Certificates of Deposit are guaranteed by the U.S. Government. They have minimal risk because the bank that offers them is insured by the Federal Deposit Insurance Corporation (FDIC). This provides you with insurance on your investment up to $100,000. However, only the principal is insured, not the interest. Savings Certificates of Deposit yield slightly higher rates of return than treasury bills. However, because income earned on Savings Certificates is fully taxable, the return is not as high as it may seem.

REAL ESTATE

There are many advantages in investing in real estate: it can be initially acquired with a cash fraction of the purchase price, there are many tax advantages, and the possibility of long term price appreciation. When you purchase real estate, most of the money is usually borrowed. The investor typically has a down payment of 15-25% of the purchase price. The interest paid on the real estate mortgage (the money borrowed for purchase) is tax deductible. Property taxes paid on real estate are also deductible from your personal income.

If your property appreciates and you have owned it for more than one year, the capital gain realized on the sale of such property is 60% tax free. Also, when selling a house that has been used as a primary place of residence, the government will not tax the gain on the sale of the house if the proceeds are used to buy another within a certain period of time.

Real estate investments are attractive; but there are disadvantages as well. In addition to the regular cash outlays for mortgage and taxes, there are insurance, maintenance, and utilities expenses. Property ownership entails certain responsibilities and certain worries—you can't tuck real estate into the safety of a bank vault. Keep in mind too that real estate is a very low liquid investment.

REAL ESTATE INVESTMENT TRUSTS

Even more than stock and money market investors, a single purchaser of real estate must initially commit large sums before he can invest at all. But just as benefits are provided for small stock and money market investors through mutual funds and money market funds, the prospective real estate investor may join a group by purchasing shares of a "real estate investment trust" (REIT). There are two types of REITs, *equity trusts* and *mortgage trusts*.

The manager of an *equity trust* actually purchases real estate properties such as shopping centers, office buildings, apartment complexes and land for the benefit of the shareholder. Most of the income comes from rents received on the property held or proceeds from a sale. The manager must be concerned that property purchased is in a desirable location to insure high occupancy and profitable resale. The *mortgage trust* provides mortgages to builders. The interest paid on these mortgages provides the shareholder with his return. With a mortgage trust there is the possibility that a mortgagee will default, thus providing the REIT with a loss of interest and possible capital loss.

REITs, treated on the stock market like ordinary corporate stock, are traded daily. This means that a REIT investor can buy and sell real estate much more quickly than any sole real estate owner attempting to buy and sell property himself.

When choosing a REIT, seriously consider its management, focusing on whether managers invest conservatively or speculatively. For more information and a list of REITs, write:

National Association Of Real Estate Investment Trusts
1101 17th Street N.W.
Washington, D.C. 20036

COMMODITIES

For investors willing to take greater risks, investment in the "commodities market" may provide large profits. Buyers and sellers use the commodities exchange to establish the market price of copper, silver, wheat, corn, and other products. A commodities investor buys or sells contracts for delivery of any of the commodities exchanged at a specified price and date. He rarely takes delivery of the actual commodity itself, because he resells the contract before its delivery date. What he actually does is speculate that the price of the goods will increase or decrease before the delivery date of his contract.

Because a commodities investor must be prepared to cover potential large losses, he must be backed by large amounts of capital. Even someone making a small initial investment must have larger sums in reserve in case he loses money. In addition, investors almost invariably need capable, alert commodities brokers to help them because commodities market prices may change very rapidly. In addition to hiring a competent broker, the investor himself must often spend long hours studying changing market conditions.

GOLD

For thousands of years gold has maintained its considerable value, surviving both political and economic strife. When paper currencies have become worthless, gold has still held its value as an exchange currency. Gold has been purchased as a hedge against inflation. To be well diversified, an investor should consider gold for his portfolio of investments.

There are six basic ways to invest in gold. One way is to buy gold coins. Coins can be purchased through currency dealers or jewelers and are very easy to store either in a safe deposit box at a bank, or at home. A very popular coin is the South African Krugerrand. It weighs exactly one ounce and since there are so many in circulation it is not sought by coin collectors. Because of these two features, the value is pegged directly to the London gold price quoted daily in the paper, and it is easily exchanged. However, when buying or selling, you will pay a commission generally between 5% and 8% over the London price. There are, of course, other gold coins in different weights that are worthy of investment consideration.

Gold coins are advantageous because they are liquid and easily divisible. But gold can be purchased in much larger quantities as ingots or bars. Gold bullion, for example, is purchased in minimum units of 2,000 ounces. The advantage of buying bullion is that the commission drops to 3%. Bullion must be stored and insured, and usually a ½% per year storage fee is charged. The price of 2,000 ounces of gold is, of course, beyond the reach of most individual investors.

Another way to own gold is by buying jewelry. The quantity of gold in jewelry varies greatly from 14 karats, which is only 58.5% fine gold, to 24 karats, which is 100% fine gold. When reselling gold that you have taken possession of, there is often an assaying fee. This fee is charged to determine the actual gold content for the purchaser. Owning jewelry, like gold coins and gold bullion, provides no current income, but with jewelry one can enjoy wearing the precious metal. It should be noted that because of the crafts-manship and other aesthetic considerations involved, gold jewelry prices are almost always higher than the weight value of the gold itself.

The three ways of owning gold just mentioned require the physical possession of gold by the investor. Actual possession may have its satisfactions, but it also entails problems of storage and security. In the remaining three, the investor never takes delivery of the gold. One such way is by buying stocks in gold-related companies. These include either U.S. or Canadian gold mining shares or American Depository Receipts (ADR) of South African mines. Gold-mining securities often pay very high dividends. To aim for such yields, the investor should look for mines with consistent high records of profitability. There is more risk involved here than in owning gold itself; the management of the company is a factor. Such an investment, though, is very liquid in that the stocks are traded on various stock exchanges.

The most speculative way of all to invest in gold is in the commodities exchanges. As was mentioned in the commodities section, contracts with promises of delivery are traded. Typically, 5% of the value of the gold controlled is put up for the initial investment. One gold contract controls 100 ounces of gold. There-fore, if the price fluctuates widely, great gains or losses are realized. Here there are no storage or insurance costs because delivery is hardly ever taken. With speculation in gold commod-ities, you have a high risk, highly liquid investment.

And lastly, there are gold certificates. A safe and convenient way to own gold is to buy a certificate that represents a specific number of ounces of gold. Some certificates require only a $100 minimum. The gold is stored in safekeeping by a financial institution. You are able to purchase gold at the current price plus a commission. Certificates permit the purchase of gold in modest quantities without taking physical possession. To cash in your investment, you simply sell your certificate, again at the current price of gold. A commission of up to 3% is charged on the purchase, and up to 1% is charged on the sale.

COLLECTIBLES

Collecting stamps, coins, oriental rugs, art, and other such assets can be an enjoyable way to make an investment. If you feel this type of investment is for you, you should either be very well informed on the subject, or have ample time to learn. You should find out the right places to buy and sell and learn who are the reputable dealers in the field. Collectibles are low liquid investments. To convert your investment to cash you will need to find the right buyer. If you need to sell quickly, you may have to compromise considerably on the price.

RETIREMENT PLANS

Because of the uncertainty about the long-range capabilities of the Social Security System and because Social Security was never intended to completely provide for anyone's future, the government has presented a few alternatives for retirement plans. These plans allow an individual to set up his own personal account. The government supports these plans by granting tax relief for the money which is set aside.

Individual Retirement Accounts. Any wage earner, including participants in employer retirement plans, may contribute up to $2,000 yearly to an "Individual Retirement Account" (IRA) and may add an additional $250 yearly for an unemployed spouse. The amount of a taxpayer's yearly IRA contributions will be deducted from his gross income for that year, and taxes will be deferred on IRA dividends, interest, and capital gains. Under retirement plans, taxes are strategically deferred until the fund is withdrawn at retirement, at which time the investor is presumably in a lower tax bracket.

IRA funds should not be withdrawn until the taxpayer reaches the age of at least 59½. Earlier withdrawal causes the funds to be treated as ordinary income and subjects them to a 10% federal penalty tax. When properly withdrawn after age 59½, however, the money will be taxed at the retired investor's current tax rate.

IRAs may be set up under either an existing bank plan or a self-directed plan. Under the former, bank or insurance company managers make all investment decisions concerning the funds, guaranteeing the investor either a fixed rate or a variable return. A variable return is based of course on the manager's investment performance.

Under a self-directing plan, the investor makes his own decisions. Some large brokerage firms allow the IRA investor to set up his account with investment in stock, bonds, or mutual funds. For an IRA investor considering a self-directing plan, the tax consequences of the investments chosen are important. For example, to an IRA bond investor, a *municipal* bond's tax free status is not helpful because taxes on an IRA investment are deferred until the funds are withdrawn. Therefore, an IRA bond investor should buy higher-yielding *corporate* bonds, leaving the untaxed municipal bonds to those investors concerned with immediate tax consequences.

Investments providing long term capital gains are not attractive to an IRA investor. Because taxes are deferred from IRA plans, the 60% tax free status of a long term capital gain is no longer helpful. The IRA investor, unlike other investors, should focus on investments providing high current interest (or dividend) income or short term capital gains.

The Keogh Plan (also known as the HR-10 plan). Very similar to the IRA plans for salaried workers, the Keogh (pronounced 'key-o") retirement plan is aimed at self-employed individuals and their employees. A participant may invest the lesser of $15,000 or 15% of his annual gross income from self-employment. If a self-employed person's adjusted gross income is not more than $15,000, he can invest a maximum amount of $750, or 100% of anything less than $750 of self-employed income. Someone both salaried and self-employed may participate in the Keogh plan on the basis of his self-employment income. For instance, someone earning an annual

$20,000 salary and $10,000 from self-employment may maintain both an IRA up to $2,000 and also contribute $1,500 (15% of $10,000) to a Keogh retirement plan.

As with IRAs, Keogh plan contributions are deducted from the individual's gross income for a given year, and taxes on the fund's income are deferred until withdrawal. Keogh funds should be withdrawn only while the taxpayer is between ages 59½ and 70½, or earlier if disabled. The Keogh investor, like the IRA investor, may withdraw money (1) in a lump sum, (2) by purchasing United States Retirement Bonds, (3) in periodic annuity payments for the period of his or her life expectancy, or (4) in a combination of the first three. For premature distributions there is a withdrawal penalty like the one for IRAs. There is a penalty tax of 10%, plus the withdrawn money is reported as ordinary income.

Employers who have Keogh retirement plans for themselves must set them up for employees who have worked at least 1,000 hours annually for three years or longer. To provide a Keogh plan for such employees, the employer must contribute the same percentage of the employees income that he shelters for himself. Thus, a 15% contributor to a Keogh plan must contribute 15% of each employee's income to a Keogh plan set up for the employee.

Annuities. Under an annuity retirement plan, an individual contracts to pay an insurance company either a lump sum or a series of "premium payments" in exchange for the company's promise to periodically pay the person a specific amount for life. In most annuity contracts, if the insured should die before age 65 the insurance company agrees to pay either the accumulated gross premiums or the cash value of the policy to the insured's beneficiary.

The annuity investor or "annuitant" may choose among several types of contracts, including "fixed dollar annuities," "variable annuities," and "joint and last survivor annuities." Under fixed-dollar annuity contracts, the company periodically pays the annuitant a fixed sum for a definite length of time agreed to in the contract. Under this plan, the annuitant always knows how much money he will receive from the insurance company for a particular period.

Under a variable plan, the annuitant receives payments that will vary. The insurance company combines money from numerous premium payments and invests it, often in common stock. The annuitant's income varies with the success of the investment, increasing and decreasing with the value of the stocks. At some investment risk, an investor in a variable plan has the chance of receiving larger annuity payments.

Under joint and last survivorship annuities, payment is made to the first annuitant at regular intervals for life. After the first annuitant dies, the second receives payment. Contracts for this type cf annuity are more expensive than those covering only a single life because the insurance company will probably make payments for a longer period of time than it would if the contract covered only one person. For those eager to provide greater security for family members who survive the family wage-earner, joint and last survivorship annuities, though more expensive, should be considered.

BASIC RULES FOR INVESTING

Your personal investments should be based on a carefully examined budget of your current and projected expenses and income. To get a clear picture of income and expenses, make out a personal income statement. (A model form is at the end of this chapter.) After filling out your income statement, examine whether or not your resources are allocated to best suit your needs. An investor should rearrange his budget as his needs and interests change. When he realizes he needs to spend more money in a particular area, such as child care, he may get the funds needed by reducing his spending for something else. As helpful as it is to have a well planned budget, this budget should not become so rigid that cash cannot be spent for recreation and unexpected opportunities as they arise.

No matter how a budget is set up, at least 5 to 10% of income should be designated as savings to be invested. A part of these savings should be set aside as an emergency fund. Your prime concern in placing this emergency money is that it be immediately available and federally insured; interest rate is a lesser consideration. Savings and loan accounts, bank accounts, and government money funds are appropriate for your emergency fund.

After depositing emergency funds, the investor should explore ways for investing the rest of his savings. No one investment vehicle is best for all investors, nor is one investment vehicle always appropriate for a particular investor. As the economy changes because of inflation, interest rates, and other factors, investors should review their investment portfolio and make appropriate changes. If interest rates are high, for example, money should be invested in any of several vehicles which bear interest.

If interest rates are likely to rise even further, investors should buy a series of short term certificates. That way they can continuously buy certificates paying higher and higher interest rates. Using the same logic, an investor who expects interest rates to fall should buy long term certificates, thus insuring the high rate even after interest rates have fallen. Bond investors must also concern themselves with interest rates. If a bond investor expects interest rates to drop, he should buy high yielding, long term bonds.

When interest rates fall, the stock market becomes a more attractive opportunity. The price of money has come down, so the higher risk of the stock market may become acceptable because the lower risk, high return on interest is no longer available.

No matter what area of investment you are involved in, two general rules apply. First, *investors should not assume their investment portfolio is unchangeable* after it has been established. A wise investment decision based on this year's interest rates might no longer be profitable if interest rates are low in one year from now. Second, *investors in all markets should diversify by holding a variety of investments.* An investor whose funds are all placed in one type of investment risks losing a large proportion of the money if that investment declines in market value. An investor with a diversified portfolio can afford minor setbacks because the profitable invesments will help to recoup any losses suffered on other investments.

FINANCIAL ADVISORS

Determining your needs. The use of a financial advisor can be very helpful. Such a person may be hired to assist you in setting up your financial plan. In deciding whether you need an advisor, consider the following questions:

- Are my assets larger than I can confidently manage?

- Do I have the time and energy to learn the details necessary for effective financial management?

- What is my investment track record up to now? Have I shown financial aptitude?

- Can I afford to make novice mistakes?

Although some people are reluctant to pay for financial advice, it should be considered that, in the long run, ineffective do-it-yourself investment could be more expensive than any advisor's fee.

How to choose a financial advisor. To choose a financial advisor, begin by seeking recommendations from your banker, lawyer, accountant, or friends. After getting the names of several advising firms, send for their brochures and carefully read and compare the information contained in them. Once you have narrowed your choices to a few firms, make an appointment with a firm representative. You should ask the representative to describe the type of clientele the firm serves. Such a description will help you estimate whether the firm often deals with people like yourself and in the investments in which you are particularly interested. It is important that the financial advisor you choose be relatively free of investment bias. An advisor should be able to consider any and all possibilities impartially. A good advisor will be interested in more than just the commissions to be earned.

In addition to asking about clientele, you should ask the representative to describe the firm's past performance, its size, date of establishment, and the individual who will advise you.

Next, seek an interview with the one who will be likely to handle your account. During this interview, you will want to discover this person's qualifications and experience, potential sensitivity to your financial needs and objectives, and willingness to spend the necessary time on your account.

In meeting with your personal representative, you should also ask about the firm's fee. Most investment advisors charge clients a percentage of the amount invested. Smaller investments are usually charged a higher percentage, or they may be handled for a flat fee.

After comparing several firms, choose the one you feel most comfortable with. Always feel free to question specific investment advice you are given. If you feel uncomfortable with a pending investment, talk to specialists in the field before deciding how you wish to proceed. For example, if your advisor suggests that you buy insurance, you might check with several insurance salesmen, comparing their ideas, before accepting any one particular policy type. By doing so, you will not only receive a variety of specific insurance advice, but will also receive general background information likely to help you decide which type of insurance is best for you.

Even after hiring an advising firm and learning to work with a particular advisor, you should not lose track of your investments. Stay informed about how each investment opportunity relates to various economic changes. You know your own needs better than any outside advisor and, although you should carefully listen to advice, final decisions about your investments should always be yours.

One key to a successful financial state is being aware of where your money comes from and where it goes. Filling out the forms on the next two pages may help you visualize your current financial status and your future goals. The forms may be reproduced for your convenience.

PERSONAL INCOME STATEMENT

ANNUAL INCOME	**CURRENT**	**PROJECTED 1 YEAR**	**PROJECTED 5 YEAR**
SALARY & WAGES			
INTEREST & DIVIDENDS			
CAPITAL GAINS			
OTHER INCOME			
1. TOTAL ANNUAL INCOME			
LESS TAXES			
FEDERAL			
STATE & LOCAL			
SOCIAL SECURITY			
2. TOTAL DEDUCTIONS			
NET INCOME			
Line 1 Total Annual Income			
minus −			
Line 2 Total Deductions			
equals =			
NET INCOME			

EXPENSES

FIXED EXPENSES			
HOUSING			
DEBT REPAYMENT			
INSURANCE			
TRANSPORTATION			
MEDICAL			
EDUCATION/TRAINING			
OTHER FIXED COSTS			
1. TOTAL FIXED COSTS			
VARIABLE EXPENSES			
FOOD			
CLOTHING			
REPAIRS/UTILITIES			
SAVINGS			
OTHER INVESTMENTS			
RECREATION			
FURNISHINGS			
GIFTS/CONTRIBUTIONS			
OTHER VARIABLE EXPENSES			
2. TOTAL VARIABLE EXPENSES			
TOTAL EXPENSES			
Line 1 Fixed Expenses			
plus +			
Line 2 Variable Expenses			
equals =			
TOTAL EXPENSES			

PERSONAL BALANCE SHEET

LIQUID ASSETS		LIABILITIES	
CASH	_____	CURRENT PAYABLES	_____
SAVINGS	_____	INSTALLMENT DEBT	_____
SECURITIES	_____	MORTGAGES	_____
CASH VALUE—INS. POLICY	_____	NOTES PAYABLE	_____
OTHER LIQUID ASSETS	_____	OTHER DEBTS	_____
TOTAL LIQUID ASSETS	_____	TOTAL LIABILITIES	_____

OTHER ASSETS

STOCKS	_____
BONDS	_____
REAL ESTATE	_____
HOME	_____
AUTO	_____
FURNISHINGS	_____
COLLECTIBLES	_____
OTHER ASSETS	_____
TOTAL OTHER ASSETS	_____

TOTAL ASSETS		NET WORTH	
TOTAL LIQUID ASSETS	_____	TOTAL ASSETS	_____
plus+		minus−	_____
TOTAL OTHER ASSETS	_____	TOTAL LIABILITIES	_____
equals=		equals=	_____
TOTAL ASSETS	_____	TOTAL NET WORTH	_____

Directory

The private organizations and government offices listed here provide information and services. Those coded with the letters "Pr" are for professionals rather than parents or consumers.

If an organization has moved, for a current address contact the Special Education Information Referral Service (formerly Closer Look), Box 1492, Washington, D.C., 20013, (202) 822-7900.

PRIVATE ORGANIZATIONS

Alexander Graham Bell Association for the Deaf
3417 Volta Place, N.W.
Washington, D.C. 20007

Allergy Foundation of America
19 West 44th Street
New York, New York 10036

American Alliance for Health, Physical Education,
Recreation and Dance (Pr)
1900 Association Drive
Reston, Virginia 22091

American Association on Mental Deficiency (Pr)
5101 Wisconsin Avenue
Washington, D.C. 20016

American Coalition of Citizens with Disabilities
1346 Connecticut Ave., N.W.
Suite 1124
Washington, D.C. 20036

American Council for the Blind
1211 Connecticut Avenue, N.W.
Washington, D.C. 20006

American Diabetes Association
600 Fifth Avenue
New York, New York 10020

American Foundation for the Blind, Inc.
15 West 16th Street
New York, New York 10011

American Occupational Therapy Association (Pr)
1383 Piccard Drive
Rockville, Maryland 20580

American Orthotic and Prosthetic Association (Pr)
1440 N Street, N.W.
Washington, D.C. 20005

American Physical Therapy Association (Pr)
1156 15th Street, N.W.
Washington, D.C. 20005

American Printing House for the Blind
P.O. Box 6085
Louisville, Kentucky 40206

American Speech and Hearing Association (Pr)
10801 Rockville Pike
Rockville, Maryland 20852

American Wheelchair Bowling Association
6718 Pinehurst Drive
Evansville, Indiana 47711

Arthritis Foundation
3400 Peachtree Road, N.E.
Suite 1101
Atlanta, Georgia 30026

Arthrogryposis Association
106 Herkimer Street
North Bellmore, New York 11710

Association for Children with Learning Disabilities
4156 Library Road
Pittsburgh, Pennsylvania 15234

Association for Education of the Visually Handicapped
206 North Washington Street
Alexandria, Virginia 22314

Canadian Association for the Mentally Retarded
Kinsmen NIMR Building
York University Campus
4700 Keele Street, Downsview
Toronto, Ontario, Canada M3J1P3

Canadian Hearing Society
60 Bedford Road
Toronto, Ontario, Canada M5R2K2

Canadian National Institute for the Blind
1929 Bayview Avenue
Toronto, Ontario, Canada M4G3F8

Canadian Rehabilitation Council for the Disabled
1 Young Street, Suite 2110
Toronto, Ontario, Canada M5E1A5

Coalition on Sexuality and Disability
122 East 23rd Street
New York, New York 10010

Columbia Lighthouse for the Blind
421 P Street, N.W.
Washington, D.C. 20005

Compassionate Friends
P.O. Box 1347
Oak Brook, Illinois 60521

Cornelia de Lange Syndrome Foundation
60 Dyer Avenue
Collinsville, Connecticut 06022

Council of Education of the Deaf (Pr)
c/o Gallaudet College
Seventh Street and Florida Avenue
Washington, D.C. 20002

Council for Exceptional Children (Pr)
1920 Association Drive
Reston, Virginia 22091

Cystic Fibrosis Foundation
6000 Executive Boulevard, Suite 309
Rockville, Maryland 20852

Dental Guidance Council for Cerebral Palsy (Pr)
122 East 23rd Street
New York, New York 10010

Disabilities Rights Center, Inc.
1346 Connecticut Ave. NW
Washington, D.C. 20036

Disabled Resource Living Center
Kinsmen Rehabilitation Foundation
2256 West 12th Street
Vancouver, British Columbia
Canada B6K2N5

Down's Syndrome Congress
1640 West Roosevelt Road
Chicago, Illinois 60608

Dysautonomia Foundation, Inc.
370 Lexington Avenue
New York, New York 10017

Ephphatha Services for the Deaf and Blind
421 South 4th Street
P.O. Box 15167
Minneapolis, Minnesota 55415

Epilepsy Foundation of America
1828 L Street, Suite 405
Washington, D.C. 20036

Federation of the Handicapped
211 West 14th Street
New York, New York 10011

Foundation for Children with Learning Disabilities
99 Park Avenue, Second Floor
New York, New York 10011

Friedreich's Ataxia Group in America
P.O. Box 1116
Oakland, California 94611

Human Resources Center
Willets Road
Albertson, New York 11507

International Association of Parents of the Deaf
814 Thayer Avenue
Silver Spring, Maryland 20910

International Spinal Cord Research Foundation (Pr)
4100 Spring Valley Road, Suite 104LB3
Dallas, Texas 75234

John Tracy Clinic
(deafness/hearing impairments, deaf-blind)
806 West Adams Boulevard
Los Angeles, California 90007

Juvenile Diabetes Association
23 East 26th Street
New York, New York 10010

Leukemia Society of America
800 Second Avenue
New York, New York 10017

Mainstream Information Center
1200 15th Street, N.W.
Washington, D.C. 20005

Muscular Dystrophy Association, Inc.
810 Seventh Avenue
New York, New York 10019

National Amputation Foundation
12-45 150th Street
Whitestone, New York 11357

National Association of the Deaf
814 Thayer Avenue
Silver Spring, Maryland 20910

National Association for Down's Syndrome
Box 63
Oak Park, Illinois 60303

National Association for Mental Health, Inc. (Pr)
1800 N. Kent Street, Second Floor
Arlington, Virginia 22209

National Association of the Deaf-Blind
2703 Forest Oak Circle
Norman, Oklahoma 73071

National Association of the Physically Handicapped
76 Elm Street
London, Ohio 43140

National Association of Private
Residential Facilities for the Mentally Retarded
6269 Leesburg Pike
Falls Church, Virginia 22044

National Association of Private Schools for
Exceptional Children
P.O. Box 34293
West Bethesda, Maryland 20817

National Association for Retarded Citizens
2709 Avenue E East
P.O. Box 6109
Arlington, Texas 76011

National Association for the Visually Handicapped
305 East 24th Street, Room 17-C
New York, New York 10010

National Ataxia Foundation
6681 Country Club Drive
Minneapolis, Minnesota 55427

National Center for a Barrier-Free Environment
1140 Connecticut Avenue
Suite 1006
Washington, D.C. 20036

National Center for Law and the Handicapped
University of Notre Dame
P.O. Box 477
Notre Dame, Indiana 46556

National Committee on Arts for the Handicapped
1825 Connecticut Avenue, N.W.
Suite 418
Washington, D.C. 20009

National Congress of Organizations of the
Physically Handicapped, Inc.
1627 Deborah Avenue
Rockford, Illinois 61103

National Easter Seal for Crippled Children and Adults
2023 West Ogden Avenue
Chicago, Illinois 60612

National Federation of the Blind
1629 K Street, N.W.
Washington, D.C. 20006

National Foundation of Dentistry for the Handicapped (Pr)
1726 Champa, Suite 422
Denver, Colorado 80202

National Foundation for Ileitis and Colitis
295 Madison Avenue
New York, New York 10017

National Foundation/March of Dimes
1275 Mamaroneck
White Plains, New York 10605

National Genetics Foundation
555 West 57th Street, Room 1240
New York, New York 10019

National Hearing Aid Society
20361 Middlebelt Road
Livona, Michigan 48152

National Hemophilia Foundation
19 West 34th Street, Room 1204
New York, New York 10001

National Institute of Mental Health
Public Inquiries, Room 9C-05
5600 Fishers Lane
Rockville, Maryland 20852

National Multiple Sclerosis Society
205 East 42nd Street
New York, New York 10017

National Neurofibomatosis Foundation
3401 Woodridge Court
Mitchelville, Maryland 20716

National Retinitis Pigmentosa Foundation
Rolling Park Building
8311 Mindale Circle
Baltimore, Maryland 21207

National Society for Autistic Children
1234 Massachusetts Avenue, N.W.
Suite 1017
Washington, D.C. 20005

National Spinal Cord Injury Group
369 Elliot Street
Newton Upper Falls, Massachusetts 02164

National Tay-Sachs and Allied Diseases Association
122 East 42 Street
New York, New York 10068

National Tuberous Sclerosis Association
P.O. Box 159
Laguna Beach, California 92651

North America Riding for the Handicapped Association, Inc.
P.O. Box 100
Ashburn, Virginia 22011

Orton Society (dyslexia)
724 York Road
Baltimore, Maryland 21204

Prader-Willi Syndrome Association
5515 Malibu Drive
Edina, Minnesota 55436

Quebec Association for Children with Learning Disabilities
1181 Mountain Street
Montreal, Quebec, Canada, H3G1Z2

Rehabilitation International USA
20 West 40th Street
New York, New York 10018

Sex Information and Education Council of the U.S. (SIECUS)
84 Fifth Avenue, Room 407
New York, New York 10001

Society for the Rehabilitation of the Facially Disfigured
560 First Avenue
New York, New York 10016

Special Citizens Futures Unlimited (autistic adults)
823 United Nations Plaza
New York, New York 10017

Spina Bifida Association of America
343 South Dearborn Street
Room 317
Chicago, Illinois 60604

Task Force on Life Safety and the Handicapped
P.O. Box 19044
Washington, D.C. 20036

Tuberous Sclerosis Association of America
P.O. Box 44
Rockland, Massachusetts 02320

United Cerebral Palsy Association, Inc.
66 East 34th Street
New York, New York 10016

United Ostomy Association
2001 West Beverly Boulevard
Los Angeles, California 90057

Western Law Center for the Handicapped
849 South Broadway, Suite M-22
Los Angeles, California 90014

GOVERNMENT AGENCIES

Administration of Developmental Disabilities
Office of Human Development Services
Department of Health and Human Services
330 Independence Avenue, S.W.
Room 3194
Washington, D.C. 20201

American Association of University Affiliated Programs
for the Developmentally Disabled (Pr)
(35 interdisciplinary facilities working with the Department of
Health, Education and Welfare)
1234 Massachusetts Avenue, N.W.
Suite 813
Washington, D.C. 20005

Architectural and Transportation Barriers Compliance Board
330 C Street, S.W.
Room 1010, Switzer Building
Washington, D.C. 20202

Special Education Information Referral Service
(formerly Closer Look)
Box 1492
Washington, D.C. 20013

National Library Service for the Blind and Physically Handicapped
Library of Congress
Washington, D.C. 20542

Office of Deafness and Communicative Disorders
Room 3416, Switzer Building
400 Maryland Avenue
Washington, D.C. 20202

Office of Special Education
Department of Education
400 Maryland Avenue, S.W.
Donahoe Building
Washington, D.C. 20202

President's Committee on Employment of the Handicapped
Department of Labor
1111 20th Street, N.W.
Washington, D.C. 20036

President's Committee on Mental Retardation
7th and D Streets SW
Washington, D.C. 20201

Special Education and Rehabilitative Services Clearinghouse
for the Handicapped
Department of Education
400 Maryland Avenue, S.W.
Switzer Building, Room 3106
Washington, D.C. 20202

Glossary

A

Account: To account for financial transactions is to provide a written statement of money earned, accrued, spent, and invested, and to explain how and why these transactions have taken place.

Age of Majority: At the age of majority a person is entitled to the management of his or her own affairs by law. The age of majority in most states is 18.

Annuity, Annuitant: An annuity is the regular payment of money for life or for a specified period of time. The receiver or beneficiary of such payments is the annuitant.

Annuties are available in many forms, but usually involve the payment of money to an organization for the promised return of one or more payments at a future time. An annuity that begins payments as soon as it is funded is sometimes referred to as an immediate annuity. An annuity that begins payments on a specified future date is sometimes called a deferred annuity.

Below are the three most common methods of annuity payments:

1. A lump sum annuity pays all money owed the annuitant at one time.

2. A fixed annuity guarantees the annuitant an unchanging amount of money regularly for a specified period of time (most commonly, for life).

3. A variable annuity pays the annuitant an amount that depends on the investment performance of the company offering the annuity.

B

Beneficiary: In general, a beneficiary is a person or institution named to receive the income and/or principal of a certain property. For example, the beneficiary named in a life insurance policy will receive the amount of the policy at the death of the insured. The beneficiary of a trust receives income and/or principal from the trust.

Bond, Bond Fee: In court a bond is an amount of money that will be forfeited if the person making the pledge does not follow through properly on his or her obligation. Such bonds are sometimes called "performance" or "surety" bonds, and certain companies or individuals (bondsmen) specialize in guaranteeing payment of these bonds in case of forfeit. The charge for such a service is called a bond fee.

C

Capital Gain or Loss: Profit (or loss) from the sale of a capital asset. Capital gains may be short term (one year or less) or long-term (more than one year).

Codicil: A codicil is a formally executed addition to or change in the terms of a will, not requiring the complete rewriting of the will.

Conservator: In some states, a conservator is the same as a full guardian of the person and the estate. In other states, a conservator is a guardian of an adult as distinguished from a guardian of a child. The conservator of an estate or of any property is appointed by the court to care for that estate or property.

D

Decedent: A decedent is a person who has died. The term is used frequently in the course of estate settlement.

Developmental Disability: Any severe chronic disability which:
    1. Is attributable to a mental or physical impairment or impairments,
    2. Manifests itself prior to age 22,
    3. Will likely continue indefinitely,
    4. Results in substantial functional limitations in three or more of the seven major life activities: a) self-care, b) receptive and

expressive language, c) learning, d) mobility, e) self-direction, f) ca-· pacity for independent living, and g) economic sufficiency, and

5. Reflects the individual's need for a combination and sequence of special services which are either of extended or life-long duration and which are individually planned and coordinated.

Distribute, Distributee: To distribute property is to pass it on to those entitled to it. For example, a probate court distributes or passes estate property on to whoever is legally entitled to it. The trustee of a trust fund distributes or passes income or principal from the trust fund to the trust beneficiary, sometimes called the distributee.

Diversify, Diversification: If investments are diversified, they are spread into several different types of properties in order to minimize the risk of loss should one investment fail. Diversification is the process of spreading investments.

Dividend: A dividend is the money or stock that the owners of a corporation's stock receive out of the corporation's profits.

E

Earned income: Earned income is wages, salaries, or fees derived from labor as opposed to income derived from invested capital such as rents, dividends, and interest.

Endowment Insurance: Endowment insurance is a type of protection which combines life insurance and investment. If the insured outlives the policy, the face value is paid to the insured. If he or she does not, the face value is paid to the beneficiary.

Estate, Probate Estate, Estate Tax: A person's estate is all the money and all the real and personal property owned by that person.

A decedent's probate estate is that part of an estate which passes through the probate court in a will.

A decedent's gross estate is the total property for estate tax purposes, and his or her adjusted gross estate or taxable estate is the gross estate less certain deductions. The estate pays an estate tax based on the taxable estate. Thus, a decedent's estate is itself a taxpayer, managed as such by an administrator or executor.

Estate Planning: Estate planning is the process of creating and preserving one's property during one's lifetime and arranging for its transfer at one's death. Most frequently, the term is associated with advantageous investment and tax planning that does not sacrifice personal and family security and welfare.

Executor: An executor is a person or institution named in a will to carry out the terms of the will.

F

Fiduciary: A fiduciary is a person or institution that takes the responsibility of acting on behalf of another person. In reference to wills, estates, and trusts, the following act in a fiduciary capacity for the maker of the will, for the estate, and for the beneficiaries: the attorney(s), executor(s), trustee(s), and any guardian(s) he or she may name. All are bound by good faith and trust.

Funded Trust: A funded trust is a trust in which assets are part of the principal and the income is used to meet various obligations of the trust.

G

Gift, Gift Tax: A gift is a voluntary transfer of money and/or property from one person to another who accepts it without giving anything in return. If the gift is to an individual or an organization not qualifying as non-profit, it may be subject to a gift tax. If such a tax is due, it is computed on the amount of money given or on the fair market value of the property given.

Guardian: A guardian is a person appointed by the court to control and manage another person's affairs and/or property. Most typically, a guardian is appointed to manage the affairs of a minor or of an adult who is incapable of looking after his or her own affairs.

   A guardian is limited in power by the court making the appointment. The guardian must submit regular accountings to the court and must follow the direction of the court at all times.

Guardian Ad Litem: A guardian ad litem is a guardian appointed by the court for the purpose and duration of a law suit or similar action.

Guardian-Discharge or Modification: Procedures for removing a guardian or a request for change in duties and powers of the guardian.

Guardian of the Estate: A person appointed by the court to handle the care, management, and investment of the estate (real and personal property) of another person, with the duty to protect and preserve such property.

Guardian-Limited: A guardian appointed to exercise care and custody of the ward and/or management of the ward's estate in a restricted sense. This restriction takes the form of a determination by the court that the disabled person is incompetent to act only in specific areas.

Guardian-Natural: The parent who is lawfully in control of a minor child; natural guardianship ceases when the child attains the age of majority.

Guardian of the Person: An individual appointed by the court to see that the disabled person has proper care and protective supervision in keeping with personal needs.

Guardian-Plenary: A person appointed by the court to exercise total legal control and management of the person, estate, or both.

Guardian-Public: A public official empowered to accept court appointment as a legal guardian.

Guardian-Successor: A legal guardian appointed by a court when an already functioning guardian dies, is removed by the court, or resigns.

Guardian-Temporary: A legal guardian appointed by a court for a temporary period of time when that court is given notice that some person is in immediate need of guardianship. A temporary guardian may be of the person, of the estate, or both.

Guardian-Testamentary: A testamentary guardian is a person designated by the last will and testament of a natural guardian.

I

Inherit: To inherit property is to receive it by will or by applicable state statutes (laws of descent or distribution) at the death of the owner of that property.

Insured: The person who obtained or who is otherwise covered by insurance on his or her health, life, or property.

Interest: Payments a borrower pays a lender for the use of money.

Inter Vivos: Made during one's lifetime (literally, between living persons). An inter vivos trust becomes effective during the creator's lifetime.

Intestate: To die intestate is to die without having a will. Intestacy is the state of being without a will. If a person dies intestate, the person's property passes to the heirs as required by the applicable state statute (the laws of descent and distribution), regardless of how the person who died may have intended the property to pass.

Invest, Investment Company: To invest is to use money to make more money.

An investment company (commonly referred to as a mutual fund) will arrange to put an individual's money to work by adding it to sums from other people and investing it on a larger and/or more diverse scale than the individual would be capable of achieving alone. The money is managed by the investment company or another company retained as its investment advisor. The company sells shares of ownership in its own company which represent ownership of its group of investments.

A "closed end" investment company or mutual fund sells only a fixed number of shares, and these are bought and sold (after the original purchase) in the open market like shares of common stock. An "open fund" investment company sells a continuous offering of shares, and the price of a share is determined by the current market value of the company's investments plus, in some cases, a sales charge (or load). Shares of an open end mutual fund may be redeemed (sold back to the company) at any time. The profits from both types of investment company come from the money they make in dividends, interest, and capital gains from their investments.

Irrevocable: Unchangeable. An irrevocable trust is a trust that cannot be changed.

Itemized Return: The tax return on which certain personal expenditures are allowed by the Internal Revenue Code as deductions from adjusted gross income as long as the taxpayer does not use the standard deduction and the total itemized deduction exceeds the zero bracket amount.

J

Joint Return: Tax return filed for federal or state taxes by a husband and wife together, each being individually liable. It includes the income of both spouses. Usually it is more beneficial for a couple to file a joint return than a separate return.

L

Least Restrictive Alternative: A policy based on the belief that persons should be free to live as they please and that when government must interfere with a person's liberty the services should be designed to maximize the developmental potential of the person and should be provided in the setting that is least restrictive of personal liberty.

Legacy, Legatee: A legacy (also known as a bequest) is a gift of personal property by will. The recipient of such a gift is the legatee.

Letters of Office: A document issued by the court indicating the appointment of a guardian of the person, a guardian of the estate, or both.

Life Estate: A person with a life estate (or life interest) in property has a right to use the property during his or her own or another designated person's lifetime.

Life Tenant: A life tenant is the person who has the use of property during his or her lifetime.

Limited Payment Insurance: Limited payment insurance is a type of life insurance for which premiums are payable for a definite period of time after which the policy is fully paid.

Liquid, Liquid Assets, Liquidate: If property is liquid, it is easily marketable or convertible to cash. Cash in hand is considered property in its most liquid form. Liquid assets are properties that can easily be marketed or converted to cash. To liquidate property generally means to convert it to cash or other easily marketable properties and then distribute the proceeds to the person or persons entitled to them.

Long-Term Debt: Any debt of a company that is due and payable more than one year hence.

M

Minor: A person who has not reached the age of majority (18 years old in most states).

Municipal Bond: A municipal bond is a certificate of debt issued (sold) by a state or local government or government agency. Generally, the interest paid to the purchaser on such bonds is exempt from federal income tax, and, with some exceptions, state and local taxes as well.

N

Non-Probate Estate: Property of a deceased person which passes to beneficiaries or persons sharing ownership in the property without being subject to the probate process.

P

Personal Property: All property owned by a person or institution except real estate.

Petitioner: A person who asks the court (a) for action or relief, or (b) to exercise its authority in some way. In guardianship proceedings, the petitioner is generally the person asking that a guardian be appointed for an alledgedly disabled person.

Portfolio: As a financial term, a person's or institution's portfolio is the total of all investments or the collection of investment assets.

Pour-Over Will: A will which directs that all, or a portion of, a testator's estate flow into an already-existing or independently established trust.

Principal: In a trust, the principal amount is all the capital, the property that produces income.

Probate, Probate Court: The court process of probate specifically involves the validation of a will as the genuine and legally acceptable last directions of the maker of the will (the testator) and the carrying out of those directions. Most commonly, a state will have a special court which handles estates and probate proceedings. This court is called probate court in most states and by other names in other states (for example, surrogate or orphans' court).

Prudent Man Rule: Trustees (as fiduciaries) must manage trust property in accordance with the prudent man rule. This requires the trustee to handle the trust property with the same care that a prudent, honest, intelligent, and diligent man would use to handle the property under the same circumstances. If a trustee is accused of mismanaging the assets, the court will often judge his conduct by applying the prudent man rule as the standard against which to measure his actions.

R

Real Property: Real property (also known as real estate or realty) is land and the buildings or other fixed improvements on that land.

Remainderman: The remainderman of a trust receives the principal (the income producing capital) of that trust when the income beneficiary or life tenant dies.

Representative Payee: A person or organization that is authorized to cash and manage public assistance checks (Social Security, Supplemental Security Income) for a person deemed incapable of doing so.

Residue, Residual (or Residuary) Clause, Residual Estate: The residue is what remains, what is left over. A residual estate is what remains of an estate after all claims and taxes have been paid and all specific distributions have been made. A residual (residuary) clause in a will arranges for the distribution of this residual property of the estate.

Respondent: The person who makes an answer to a bill or other proceeding in court. In guardianship proceedings, the respondent is the person for whom a guardian has been requested.

Revocable: Changeable. A revocable trust is a trust that can be changed.

S

Short-Term Debt: Any debt of a company that is due and payable in less than one year's time.

Spendthrift Clause: Also known as "Protection from Claims by Strangers," a spendthrift clause in a trust agreement provides that the named beneficiary has a right to trust income only and thus cannot voluntarily dispose of the capital assets (principal) of the trust or the income before it is earned and paid. As a result the trust principal and unpaid income are protected from creditors of the beneficiary.

Sprinkling, Sprinkle and Spray Trust: A provision for "sprinkling" in a trust agreement allows the trustee to use personal judgment in distributing income from the trust fund. He or she controls the timing and the amount of the distributions and decides which beneficiaries will receive those distributions. A trust with such a provision is sometimes referred to as a "sprinkle and spray" trust.

Statute: A law.

Straight Life Insurance: With straight life insurance, premiums remain the same for as long as the insured lives.

Stocks: Certificates representing ownership in a corporation; they may yield dividends, and can increase or decrease in value.

Surety: Surety is a financial guarantee that an act will be carried out or that a debt will be paid by another person. To post bond is to provide such surety.

Successor: A successor is one who follows another in a particular office. For example, a successor guardian is a person named to follow the originally named guardian if the originally named individual or institution can no longer hold office.

T

Tax-Exempted Securities: Obligations issued by a state or municipality whose interest payments (but not profits via purchase or sale) are exempted from federal taxation. The interest payment may be exempted from local taxation, too, if purchased by a state resident.

Tax Shelter: A tax shelter is an investment in property designed to reduce the tax liability on income from other sources by providing deductions that can be taken against that other income. Depreciation deductions on real property are commonly used in this fashion; these deductions (and thus property) shield or shelter income from other property from increased taxation by providing a paper loss that can be subtracted from the other income.

Term Insurance: Term insurance is a form of pure life insurance having no cash surrender value and generally furnishing insurance protection for only a specified or limited period of time, though term insurance is usually renewable from term to term.

Testament, Testamentary Capacity: A person's testament is the final disposition of his or her personal property. Anything that is testamentary relates to a will. Testamentary capacity is the legal competence to make a will.

Trust: Property in trust is held and managed by a person or institution (the trustee) for the benefit of those persons or institutions for whom the trust was created (the beneficiaries). The creator of a trust is commonly referred to as the settlor, grantor, or trustor.

Trust Property: Trust property is the principal amount (the corpus or body) of a trust. It is the income-producing property of a trust.

U

Unearned Income: Unearned income is income earned from investments, rental property, etc., as distinguished from income derived from labor.

W

Ward: A person, either a minor or a disabled individual, placed by a court under the care of a guardian.

Will: A will is a legal document by which an individual can direct to whom his or her property will pass at death.

Y

Yield: The yield of an investment is the amount of money it pays to the owner annually, usually expressed as a percentage of the principal value of the investment.

Z

Zero Bracket Amount: Tax law gives each individual taxpayer a flat deduction called the "zero bracket amount." This amount varies depending upon the taxpayer's filing status. The taxpayer does not have to compute this amount. It is already incorporated into the tax rate schedules and the tax table as the lowest tax brackets, with each such bracket carrying a zero tax rate.

Bibliography

Annot., 92 A.L.R. 2d 838 (1963).

Breslin, Kevin; Ganski, Linda; Hoff, Elaine; Maslov, Debbi. *A Parent's Guide to Guardianship for Developmentally Disabled Adults*. Chicago, Ill.: Illinois Association for Retarded Citizens, 6 North Michigan Ave., 1979.

Bryant, David R.; Cleveland, Michael G.; Garbutt, Stuart; Grippando, Thomas; Karey, Jennie C.; Krane, David; Mancini, Susan; McHugh, Gregory; Meltzer, Wendy; Samuels, Barbara L.; Scheller, Arthur M., Jr.; Soltman, Nelson A.; Spector, Deborah; Weill, James D. *Counseling Senior Citizens and the Handicapped*. Springfield, Ill.: Illinois Institute of Continuing Legal Education, 2395 West Jefferson, 1982.

Crown, *Planning for Emotionally Disabled Beneficiaries,* 119 T & E 38 (1980).

"Estate Planning for Families of the Mentally Disabled," *Pact Journal*. Vol. I. No. 2. Chicago, Ill.: 6 North Michigan Ave., 1982.

Frolik, *Estate Planning for Parents of Mentally Disabled Children,* 40 U. PITT. L. R. 305 (1979).

Ganski, Linda; Kerns, Elizabeth; Schub, Ora; Seider, Greig; Sitter, Susan; Smith, Susannah; Winter, Wallace. *Manual on Legal Rights and Responsibilities of Developmentally Disabled Persons in Illinois*. Springfield, Ill.: Illinois Developmental Disabilities Advocacy Authority, One West Old State Capitol Plaza.

Garrett, Jon R., *Planning A More Secure Future*. Lansing, Michigan: Michigan Association for Retarded Citizens, 416 Michigan National Tower, 1979.

"Guardianship for Mentally Disabled Adults," *Pact Journal*. Vol. 1. No. 1. Chicago, Ill.: 6 North Michigan Ave., 1982.

Hodgson, *Guardianship of Mentally Retarded Persons: Three Approaches to a Long Neglected Problem,* 37 ALB. L. REV. 407 (1973).

Kindred, M.; Cohen, J.; Penrod, D.; Shaffer, T. (eds.). *The Mentally Retarded Citizen and the Law.* New York: MacMillan Publishing Co., 1976.

Massey, *Protecting the Mentally Incompetent Child's Trust Interest from State Reimbursement Claims,* 58 DENVER L. J. 557 (1981).

National Association for Retarded Citizens, *How to Provide for Their Future,* Arlington, Tex.: P.O. Box 6109, 2709 Avenue E East, 1978.

Note, *Avoiding An Unwanted Invasion of Trust,* 45 ALBANY L. REV. 237 (1980).

Park, Clara Claiborne, and Shapiro, Leon N., M.D. *You Are Not Alone.* Boston: Little, Brown and Co., 1975.

Speir, *Estate Planning and Resource Maximization for the Elderly: Qualifying for Federal Need-based Benefits,* 74 CLEARING-HOUSE REV. 767 (1977).

Speisman, "Payment Responsibility for Medical Services Rendered in Illinois Public Mental Health Institutions." *Illinois Bar Journal,* March 1982, pp. 450-453.

Stohman, *Legal Planning for the Mentally Retarded: Guidelines for Lawyers,* 110 IDAHO L. REV. 245 (1974).

United Cerebral Palsy Association. *Digest of Federal and State Laws Concerning the Disabled.* New York City, New York: 321 W. 44th Street, 1966.

U.S. Department of Education. The Office of Information and Resources for the Handicapped. 1980. *Pocket Guide to Federal Help for the Disabled Person.* Washington, D.C.: Government Printing Office.

U.S. Department of Health and Human Services. Social Security Administration. 1982. *A Guide to Supplemental Security Income.* SSA Publication No. 05-11015.

Index

A

Accounting, 26, 70
    final, 13
Advocacy, 36
Annuities, 134, 157-158
Attorney, selection of, 3-5

B

Balance sheet, 163
Beneficiary, 12, 60, 134
Bonds, 149

C

Cash value, 135
Certificates of Deposit, 151
Collectibles, 155
Commodities, 152
Co-Trustees, *See* Trustee
Creator, 61

D

E

F

G

H

I

T